The British Television
Location Guide

Splendid
BOOKS

The British Television
Location Guide

Steve Clark and Shoba Vazirani

Contents

For Nicola, Thomas and Ellen

and for Andy, Imogen, Harry and Abigail

The British Television Location Guide

Written by Steve Clark and Shoba Vazirani

Copyright © 2014 Splendid Books Limited

The right of Splendid Books Limited to be identified as the Author of the work has been asserted by them in accordance with the Copyright, Designs and Patents Act 1988.

Splendid Books Limited
The Old Hambledon Racecourse Centre
Sheardley Lane
Droxford
Hampshire
SO32 3QY

www.splendidbooks.co.uk

British Library Cataloguing in Publication Data is available from The British Library

ISBN: 978-1-909109-02-5

Designed by Chris Fulcher at Swerve Creative
www.swerve-creative.co.uk

Printed and bound in Great Britain

Every effort has been made to fulfil requirements with regard to reproducing copyright material. The writers and publisher will be glad to rectify any omissions at the earliest opportunity. Although extensive checks have been made to ensure that all details contained in this book are correct at the time of going to press, readers may wish to confirm directions and opening times before setting out on a long journey.

Introduction

There can't be many of us who haven't at some point while watching a television series, thought: "I wonder where that was filmed?"

Well, hopefully this book will answer many of those questions. *The British Television Location Guide* can be enjoyed by those viewers who do their location spotting from their armchairs or by the more adventurous who prefer to go out and visit some of the wonderful places they've seen on screen.

From the splendour of Highclere Castle in Newbury, the setting for *Downton Abbey*, to the streets of Bristol where most of *Only Fools and Horses* was filmed, the book has something for everyone. Television companies go to great lengths to find perfect locations for their series and often the places they choose aren't well known, so among them are some of the best-kept secrets of the British countryside and its heritage.

While the majority of the locations and places featured in this book are open to the public, there are some that belong to private individuals. We're sure our readers will remember this and respect that these properties are out of bounds.

Happy location hunting!

Steve Clark and Shoba Vazirani

Castle
10 mile

bbey

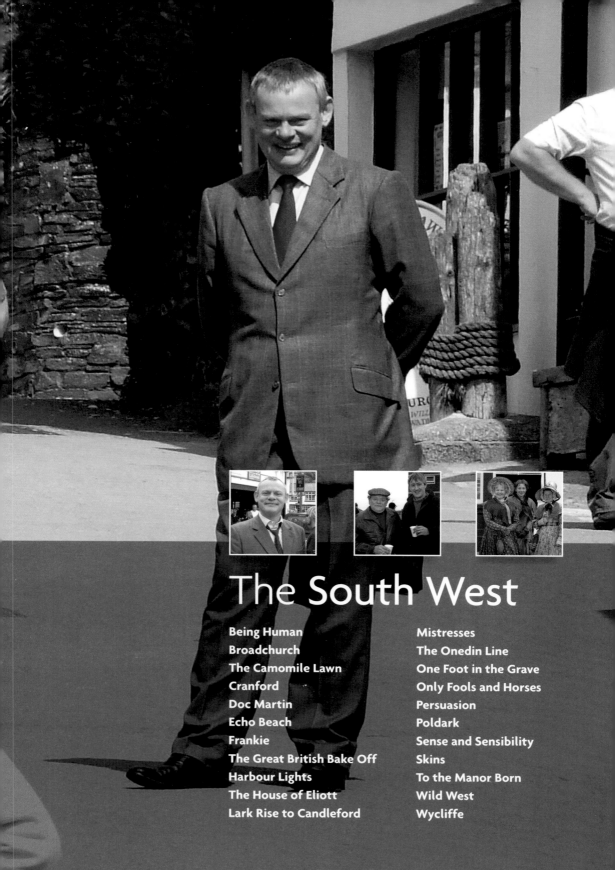

The South West

Being Human	Mistresses
Broadchurch	The Onedin Line
The Camomile Lawn	One Foot in the Grave
Cranford	Only Fools and Horses
Doc Martin	Persuasion
Echo Beach	Poldark
Frankie	Sense and Sensibility
The Great British Bake Off	Skins
Harbour Lights	To the Manor Born
The House of Eliott	Wild West
Lark Rise to Candleford	Wycliffe

Being Human
Bristol

This supernatural drama about three 20-something housemates who also happened to be a ghost, a vampire and a werewolf, quickly captured the imagination of a huge audience when the pilot was screened in 2008. The first two series were shot virtually entirely on location in Bristol, a city popular with production companies thanks to its diverse scenery. The famous Clifton Suspension Bridge was easy to spot as were scenes filmed in upmarket Clifton Village.

The home of Annie, Mitchell and George was located at Windsor Terrace in Totterdown, an iconic area in the city with multi-coloured houses terraced down some of the steepest hills in the country. A private house was used to shoot exteriors while interiors were filmed on set. The pub the characters were seen drinking in is also located in Windsor Terrace, while Bristol General Hospital was used to film Mitchell and George's place of work and where the romance blossomed between George and Nina. A terrifying scene where Mitchell (Aidan Turner) renewed his blood-lust was shot in a hotel room in the Mercure Holland House.

The producers of the show, which ended in March 2013, were attracted to Bristol's variety of architecture, particularly some of its older buildings which lent a gothic feel, perfect for a drama like *Being Human*. What's more, it was able to take advantage of the city's close proximity to Cardiff where series three to five were filmed, although the house used for the main characters' home was actually a property in Cannon Street, Barry.

Above: (top) Filming *Being Human*, *(bottom)* Aidan Turner as Mitchell

Sat nav references:

Bristol General Hospital (BS1 6SY)
Mercure Holland House (BS1 6SQ)

Broadchurch
West Bay

The seaside resort of West Bay in Dorset buzzed with excitement in the summer of 2012 as a 60-strong production crew descended to film the first series of this gripping eight-part ITV1 drama starring David Tennant and Olivia Colman.

Written by Chris Chibnall, who lives in Bridport, the stunning Jurassic coastline with its dramatic cliffs, changing seas and idyllic beaches, was very much a part of the story which explored what happened to a small community when tragedy struck.

Also starring Jodie Whittaker and Pauline Quirke, the whole of fictional Broadchurch was rocked when the body of 11-year-old Danny Latimer was discovered at the foot of cliffs on a popular beach in the opening episode. This scene

Above: Detective Sergeant Ellie Miller (Olivia Colman) and Detective Inspector Alec Hardy (David Tennant) on the beach in *Broadchurch*, *Opposite:* The cast of *Broadchurch* in a publicity still.

was filmed on the East Beach at West Bay, indeed much of the series was shot in the small harbour town with the remainder filmed in Clevedon near Bristol.

The show has had a significant boost to tourism in West Bay. "We're really busy right now which is definitely connected to the popularity of *Broadchurch* and it will only increase if they do another series," said Tim Gibb, who manages the Watch House Café which can be found at the bottom of the cliff. Although no filming took place inside the premises, the café could be spotted on screen in the background. What's more, it was often frequented by Chris Chibnall who sat sipping coffee while tweaking episodes of the gripping drama during shooting. Just 20 or so yards away from the café is the Methodist Church. In the drama it doubled up as the Sea Brigade Hall and not far away is The Harbour Newsagents, used as the exterior of its Broadchurch equivalent.

On one side of the harbour is the Ellipse Caffe where some scenes were shot. Off-screen, Ellipse played host to a charity evening on the night the long-awaited final episode was screened. Customers cheered as the closing credits were played over scenes of West Bay and nearby Lyme Bay. Next door is a building called The Folly, which was used on screen as the exterior of Broadchurch police station. The ground floor of the building is currently used for storage while the first and top floors are privately-owned apartments. Indeed, when the penthouse was put on the market after filming, the seller was apparently inundated with more *Broadchurch* fans wanting to see where the show was filmed, than genuine potential buyers! And recently, a sign has been erected outside the building informing visitors that it doubled up as Broadchurch police station, in case there was any doubt. The interior of the police station and the bedrooms of Beth and Mark Lamiter and Tom Miller were created in a studio.

A mile along the top of the cliffs from where Danny's body was discovered is Freshwater Caravan Park, already popular with visitors. On screen, Pauline Quirke's oddball character Susan Wright lived there, although her actual caravan was specially brought in by the production team so can't be rented out. Along the cliffs at Eype - around a mile from West Bay - is the hut where Danny is thought to have suffered his fate. While the building itself is a privately owned holiday home, there is a small, pretty beach which is worth a visit.

The cast and crew stayed at The Bull, a 16th Century hotel in West Bay. Marketing manager Billy Lintell was thrilled to welcome her well-known guests. "We knew *Broadchurch* was going to be big because of the star-studded line up and we know Chris Chibnall as he lives locally so we had high hopes," she revealed.

"What's amazing is how the secret of whodunit was so closely guarded. Apparently, the cast weren't allowed to drink in case they blabbed. I can tell you though that we have a lovely cocktail bar in the hotel and they definitely used it!"

The show's creator and writer Chris Chibnall, whose other credits include *Doctor Who*, *Torchwood* and *Law and Order*, described *Broadchurch* in part as "a love letter to the landscape of West Dorset, where I've lived for the best part of a decade. The landscape in it forms the drama: the cliffs, the sea, the beach are all key elements of the story. I've put dinosaurs on spaceships (on screen, not in life, that would be ridiculous), but nothing has given me the satisfaction of seeing the Jurassic Coast on screen in all weathers, all times of day and night. Our cast and crew adored Dorset too - especially in the high sun of early September. Oh, they loved me, then. At the end of November, at 2am on a cliff side battered by wind and sea-spray, less so."

"Filming on location is always a challenge," said producer Richard Stokes. "If you're in a studio you have control over the elements and everything is contained in one purpose built room. Step outside and you lose all that control.

"You can be affected by the weather, the environment and the public. However, the advantage of stepping outside is the look of authenticity. You can't build the Jurassic coastline in a studio, you have to go there and film within that space. And that's what we did. As a result we hopefully have a show that looks like the whole thing takes place in our fictional world of Broadchurch on the South Coast.

"When the weather was kind we were able to shoot for a week in glorious sunshine which was all we needed to suggest the first two

Above: David Tennant as Detective Inspector Alec Hardy at the murder scene. *Below:* Detective Sergeant Ellie Miller (Olivia Colman) and Detective Inspector Alec Hardy (David Tennant) at the murder scene. *Opposite:* The stunning cliffs at West Bay.

episodes were at the height of a wonderful British summer. At its worst the November storms drove us off the side of a cliff - we couldn't raise lights, the actors were in danger so we had to decamp from the South Coast and head back to Bristol to do some interior scenes until the storms abated."

The Somerset town of Clevedon near Bristol was also used for much of the filming but on screen it all looked seamless as Broadchurch so unless you live in one of the locations you wouldn't even have noticed where West Bay ended and Clevedon began. Hill Road in Clevedon was used as Broadchurch High Street with a former branch of the NatWest bank being used as the Trader's Hotel with additions from the props team like fake menu boards and signs. Interior scenes for the hotel were filmed 25 miles away at the Bowlish House (www.bowlishhouse.com) in Shepton Mallet. The Co-op supermarket and car park in Portishead were used for a scene and the Weston-Super-Mare Hospital and Uphill Boat Yard also made appearances.

St Andrew's Church off Old Church Road in Clevedon played Broadchurch Parish Church, while the sports day scene was shot at Yeo Moor Primary School in Kennaway Road. The interior of Alexandra News in Alexandra Road was used as the inside of the newsagent's shop run by Jack Marshall (David Bradley) and the disused Seeley's newsagents building was brought back to life as the offices of the Broadchurch Echo newspaper.

Sat nav references:

Alexandra News (BS21 7QE)
Bowlish House (BA4 5JB)
Co-op Supermarket, Portishead (BS20 8LR)
Ellipse Caffe (DT6 4GZ)
Freshwater Caravan Park (DT6 4PT)
Hill Road, Clevedon (BS21 7NZ)
St Andrew's Church (BS21 7UE)
The Bull (DT6 3LF)
The Harbour Newsagents (DT6 4EN)
The Methodist Church (DT6 4EN)
Uphill Boatyard (BS23 4XR)
Watch House Café (DT6 4EN)
Weston-Super-Mare Hospital (BS23 4TQ)
Yeo Moor Primary School (BS21 6JL)

Above: **Broom Parc** has stunning views of the sea.

The Camomile Lawn
Veryan

Fans of the 1992 Channel Four drama *The Camomile Lawn* will be delighted to know that they can actually stay at Broom Parc, the attractive Edwardian cliff top house that was used for the series, as Keith and Lindsay Righton who live there run it as a bed and breakfast. The house, which was built in 1908 and is actually owned by the National Trust, enjoys stunning sea views. For more details see www.broomparc.co.uk

Sat nav references:

Broom Parc (TR2 5PJ)

Cranford
Lacock

Thanks to a star-studded cast including Oscar-winning Hollywood actress Dame Judi Dench, sensitive writing and meticulous attention to detail, this stunning costume drama was an instant success when it was screened by the BBC in 2007.

The five-part series, set in a small Cheshire market town in the 1840s, was based on three novels by Elizabeth Gaskell: *Cranford, My Lady Ludlow* and *Mr Harrison's Confessions* and followed the small absurdities and major tragedies in the lives of the people of Cranford.

Above: The ladies of Cranford from left to right – Miss Jenkyns (Dame Judi Dench), Miss Dillon (Mary Smith), Miss Pole (Imelda Staunton) and Mrs Forrester (Julia McKenzie).

It was so popular that it returned for two further episodes shown at Christmas 2009. Ideally, the production team would have loved to use the town of Knutsford in Cheshire to film *Cranford*. After all, this was Gaskell's original model. But the cost of disguising 21st Century modernisation proved too high and they had to look elsewhere to shoot.

Eventually Lacock in Wiltshire, which has been used for the *Harry Potter* films and dramas including *Pride and Prejudice, Moll Flanders* and *Emma*, was chosen as it is owned by the National Trust and outwardly displays few trappings of modern living. Indeed, visitors to Lacock have remarked how wandering through the stunning village on the southern edge of the Cotswolds is like stepping back into the 18th Century with its stone and thatched cottages and absence of road markings.

Above: (left) Dame Judi Dench and Imelda Staunton share a joke during filming, *(centre and right)* two views of Cranford sets where attention to detail was crucial in bringing the series to life.

"Because the National Trust looks after it there are no telephone poles or television aerials in sight so there was no need for us to remove those kinds of things before we started filming," explained *Cranford's* creator Sue Birtwistle who was delighted with the find.

"We just had to cover the ground [to conceal the tarmac], hide various bits of front doors, redress windows and build the front of Johnson's, Cranford's new stores, over the front of the local pub."

The village is within easy reach of Chippenham, Wiltshire by road and rail and boasts Lacock Abbey, a medieval cloistered abbey converted into the splendid country home of William Henry Fox Talbot, who discovered the photographic process, and the Fox Talbot Museum where you can trace the history of photography.

In the centre of the village in the High Street is the 18th Century Red Lion Inn (01249 730456) which was perfectly transformed into Johnson's Stores by the BBC where Miss Matty (Dame Judi) and Miss Deborah Jenkyns (Eileen Atkins) were regularly seen shopping. Other streets in Lacock were also used to double up as stores in the drama, while some villagers even gave up their homes for various scenes.

The National Trust's stunning West Wycombe Park in West Wycombe, Buckinghamshire doubled as Lady Ludlow's home, Hanbury Court. The 18th Century home of Sir Francis Dashwood, founder of the notorious Hellfire Club, it is one of England's finest theatrical houses and with its lavish interiors and fine painted ceilings it has proved the perfect setting for other productions including *Vanity Fair* and *The Importance of Being Earnest*. Telephone 01494 755571 for information about tours.

While making the journey to West Wycombe why not also pop along to the nearby village of Radnage, also within the Chiltern Hills and easily accessible from junction 5 of the M40 motorway? Here you'll find the 13th Century-built St Mary's Church which was used in the serial as Cranford Church.

On the edge of the Chiltern Hills is the splendid Ashridge Estate, an area of open countryside and woodland belonging to the National Trust which was used to shoot *Cranford's* May Day scenes, while many of the stunning garden shots were obtained at the Trust's Winkworth Arboretum at Godalming in Surrey. Telephone 01494 755557 for further information on the Ashridge Estate and 01483 208477 for opening arrangements at the Arboretum.

Cranford returned to our screens for Christmas 2009 and this time the script, again penned by Heidi Thomas, was garnered from a number of Gaskell's stories. Lacock starred as Cranford again while West Wycombe Park, Radnage, Syon House and Wasing Park were also revisited.

Anyone wondering where the steam train scenes were filmed may be interested to learn it was actually on the Foxfield Light Railway in Staffordshire, a preserved line originally built in 1893. See www.foxfieldrailway.co.uk for further details.

Sat nav references:

Ashridge Estate (HP4 1LT)
Foxfield Light Railway (ST11 9BG)
Lacock (SN15 2LG)
Red Lion Inn (SN15 2LQ)
St Mary's Church (HP14 4DU)
Syon House (TW7 6AZ)
Wasing Park (RG7 4NG)
Winkworth Arboretum (GU8 4AD)

Above: Turning back the clock - but Lacock didn't need too much work done to make it the perfect place to double as Cranford, *(above middle)* Philip Glennister as Mr Carter.

Doc Martin
Port Isaac

Picturesque Port Isaac on the north Cornwall coast has always been a favourite destination for tourists but now it has extra appeal thanks to the success of ITV's hit drama series *Doc Martin*. The show has been running on ITV1 fairly regularly since 2004 with the latest series going to air in autumn 2013. However, the lead character played by Martin Clunes, really made his first appearance in the 2000 feature film Saving Grace as Dr Martin Bamford. A year later, he appeared in two prequels – *Doc Martin* and *Doc Martin and the Legend of the Cloutie* – but became curmudgeonly Dr Martin Ellingham, a former high-flying London surgeon who swapped surgery for general practice in the sleepy fictional hamlet of Portwenn from 2004 onwards.

Port Isaac is a fabulous place and most of the village has been seen in *Doc Martin* at some point. Most notable to location hunters is Fern Cottage - Doc Martin's surgery in the series - up on the left on Roscarrock Hill. The building is

Above: **Martin Clunes and Caroline Catz pictured during a break in filming in Port Isaac.**

clearly visible from pretty much everywhere in Port Isaac, but remember - it is a private house and only the exterior is used for filming (interior scenes are filmed on sets built inside a barn on a farm outside the village, which can't be visited) and there is a sign in the garden requesting that people do not peer through the windows.

At the bottom of Roscarrock Hill and best viewed from the other side of the harbour, is the stunning waterside house that doubles up as Bert's place. Directly opposite, on the other side of the harbour in Fore Street, is the Old School Hotel and Restaurant (www.theoldschoolhotel.co.uk) the village's former school which is now a hotel. The car park doubles as the playground of Portwenn School in the series. (Interiors of the school are filmed a few miles away at Delabole Community Primary School.) Portwenn School is run by headmistress Louisa Glasson - Caroline Catz - whose will-they, won't-they relationship with the Doctor keeps viewers intrigued. Nearby is the Boathouse Stores which has appeared in the show and a few doors up from the hotel is the privately-owned home which used to play Louisa's cottage. Of course she has now moved into the surgery with the Doc and their young son.

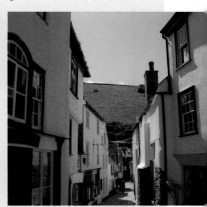

Above: (left) Doc Martin's house, Fern Cottage, *(centre)* The Old School House Hotel that is used as Louisa's school and *(right)* the narrow streets in the village make driving tricky.

The roads in Port Isaac are very narrow and you might want to consider parking at the top of the hill and walking down to the harbour. If you do decide to venture down by car then, if the tide is out, you can park on the beach – but keep an eye on the tide! Why not visit the Fish Cellars where the Doc and other residents are seen onscreen buying their fish? And there are plenty of decent places to eat at the harbour with everything from a cup of tea to a full culinary experience on offer. Among the places to eat is The Golden Lion pub, which doubles as The Crab and Lobster (www.goldenlionportisaac.co.uk) or why not try The Slipway Hotel on the harbour front in Fore Street (www.portisaachotel.com) While no filming takes place actually inside the premises, fans will have no doubt spotted the hotel's blue and white canopy in many scenes, particularly those filmed in the chemist shop which is opposite as the camera pans round.

When not being used for filming, the 'chemist', which can be found at the bottom of Fore Street which runs into Church Hill, is actually Pride of Place Fudge Shop (also known as Buttermilk) which is extremely popular with customers often happy to queue to sample the homemade treats. Not far away also in Fore Street but at the top of the village as you walk from the car park is Stowaway Tea Shoppe which is renowned for its homemade cakes and cream teas. It doubled as the florist in series three of *Doc Martin*. While the Stowaway no longer appears on screen, it is the only official stockist of *Doc Martin* merchandise in Port Isaac and has a Facebook page keeping fans updated with filming dates.

Much of *Doc Martin* is filmed in Port Isaac but another regular location to look out for is pretty Port Gaverne, the next bay along from Port Isaac. It's here that a privately-owned property called Beach House is used to play the police station.

Above: Martin Clunes as *Doc Martin* with his screen son

Other locations used for the series include Dinnaboard Farm at St Teath which played the Doc's Aunt Joan's farm and Doyden Castle (which can rented out through National Trust Cottages). This was used for the scene when the baby was abducted at the end of series five, Pencarrow House near Bodmin was the scene of the Doc and Louisa's first date and is open to the public (www.pencarrow.co.uk).

Elsewhere, The Royal Cornwall Hospital in Truro has been used for various hospital scenes, Camelot Castle Hotel in stunning Tintagel has appeared a couple of times (www.camelotcastle.com). Padstow was used when Aunt Joan's old flame John Slater (John Alderton) moored his boat there in the first series.

Lanteglos Church in Lanteglos, near Camelford, was used for the exterior of the Doc and Louisa wedding which didn't happen during series three (the interior was St Mabyn Church in St Mabyn). The Parish Church of St Winwaloe at Gunwalloe was used for Aunt Joan's funeral (although the interior was St Genny's Church at Crackington Haven) and the baby was delivered in a scene filmed at The Old Inn (www.theoldinnandrestaurant.co.uk) in St Breward. St Nonna's Church at Altarnun near Bodmin was used as the location for the wedding in series six in 2013.

Above (top) **Louisa Glasson (Caroline Catz) and Al Large (Joe Absolom),** *(middle):* **Bert Large (Ian McNeice)** *(above)* **Martin Clunes shares a joke with a member of the film crew.**

Echo Beach
Watergate Bay

The 2008 ITV drama starring Martine McCutcheon and Jason Donovan was set in the fictional Cornish town of Polnarren. In actual fact it was filmed in Looe, Polperro and Watergate Bay. Jason Donovan's character's surfboard shop and café was filmed at the Extreme Store, part of the hotel at Watergate Bay (www. watergatebay.co.uk) where scenes were also filmed at its outside bar area. Some of the stars stayed there during filming.

Sat nav references:

Watergate Bay (TR8 4AA)

Frankie
Bristol

The BBC drama *Frankie* was first screened in the spring of 2013 and followed the home and work life of a dedicated district nurse, played by Eve Myles. It was actually set in Bristol, where it was filmed, and the buildings used for both the medical practice Frankie worked at and the district nurses' office were real former NHS mental health service premises. The building used for the medical practice – the Clifton Fields Health Centre - was The Speedwell Centre, Whitefield Road and the office building used was in Clifton. Other locations used include modern flats by the floating harbour and houses in Totterdown.

The Great British Bake Off
East Harptree

This BBC baking competition took everyone by surprise when the first series, screened in 2010, became an instant hit and inspired viewers everywhere to dig out their cake tins and baking powder. It also turned judge Paul Hollywood, a professional baker, into an unlikely sex symbol while fellow judge, veteran cookery writer Mary Berry, is now a fashion icon.

Each week, 12 amateur bakers are put through their paces as they try and meet three challenges, with at least one contestant facing elimination by the end of the show. The first series saw the rounds being filmed at various locations nationwide. The second series which was screened in 2011 and went on to win a BAFTA, was filmed entirely at Valentines Mansion in Ilford, Redbridge. This Grade II listed building dating back to the 17th Century, boasts stunning gardens which proved the perfect backdrop for the *Bake Off* marquee. Love Productions, which makes the show, returned to the venue in 2012 to shoot *The Great Sport Relief Bake Off* and *The Great Comic Relief Bake Off*, screened in January 2013. Go to www.valentinesmansion.com for more information and to learn about opening times for visitors.

The third series moved to Harptree Court, a country house bed and breakfast in East Harptree close to Bristol. Guests staying in one of the beautifully appointed rooms in April, May and June 2012 were surprised to be greeted by presenter Mel Giedroyc or to spot one of the judges wandering through the gardens.

Owner Linda Hill was delighted to host the film crew for 10 weeks, although she wasn't the least bit surprised to receive a call asking to shoot there. "We've had quite a bit of filming at Harptree for shows such as *Skins*, *Casualty* and even the McFly Christmas video and we always get a call just a few weeks before they want to come," she explained. "Having the *Bake Off* team was fantastic, just like having an extension to our family and great fun for us all." Telephone 01761 221729 to make a reservation or go to www.harptreecourt.co.uk to learn more about this luxury venue.

Sat nav references:

Harptree Court (BS40 6AA)
Valentines Mansion (IG1 4XA)

Harptree Court (above) proved such a successful filming location that the production team returned to the venue to shoot series four in 2013 and the *Great Sport Relief Bake Off* which was screened in January 2014.

Harbour Lights
West Bay

The BBC drama *Harbour Lights* was expected to be a roaring success when it hit our screens in 1999 due to its star, *Heartbeat's* Nick Berry. Sadly, despite the pretty setting, it failed to impress viewers and was axed after two series. Berry played harbourmaster Mike Nicholl, an ex-Royal Navy Lieutenant Commander now in charge of the harbour of a small south coast town called Bridehaven where feuding families, ruthless business dealings and the sea dominated the lives of the people who worked and played there. The quaint real-life 16th Century Bridport Arms Hotel (www.bridportarms. co.uk) close to the sea, was one of the show's key locations and actually played two different places in the series.

Sat nav references:

Bridport Arms Hotel (DT6 4EN)

The House of Eliott
Bristol

Modern day Bristol played 1920s London for the BBC's drama *The House of Eliott*, which was broadcast between 1991 and 1994. The city was chosen to double as the capital because it was easier and cheaper to film outside London and the houses in parts of Bristol fitted the bill.

The exterior of Beatrice and Evangeline's (Stella Gonet and Louise Lombard) House of Eliott design studio was filmed at number 24 Berkeley Square. The Bristol branch of Coutts, in Corn Street, was used as fictional Gillespie Saroyan Bank and Clifton Girls School played home to Jack's apartment. The Wills Memorial Building at Bristol University also played the interior of the Houses of Parliament and the former Will's Cigarette Factory was used as Jack's film studio. Royal Fort House in Royal Fort Gardens played the offices of a rival fashion house, Hauseurs. Clifton Hill House, a university hall of residence, was used for a dinner party scene and the Orangery at another hall of residence, Goldney House doubled as a tea shop. Just across the River Avon at Leigh Woods is Leigh Court, a former mental hospital, which was used on the programme to play the interior of the Houses of Parliament, the interior of Buckingham Palace and the foyer of the Ritz Hotel.

Lark Rise to Candleford
Tetbury

The first series of this charming and heartwarming drama was shot in 2007 and screened by the BBC the following year, much to the delight of Sunday evening viewers. Flora Thompson's autobiographical novel *Lark Rise to Candleford* was beautifully adapted by Bill Gallagher and won critical acclaim for its stunning depiction of the English countryside.

Sadly, despite impressive viewer ratings, the BBC decided the fourth series of *Lark Rise to Candleford* was to be the last and the drama bowed out on February 13 2011, leaving fans wishing there could be more.

The drama was set in Lark Rise, a small Oxfordshire hamlet and the

Above: The amazing set the BBC built for the filming of *Lark Rise to Candleford*.

neighbouring market town of Candleford and examined the lives of workers and gentry as the 19th Century drew to a close. Their everyday comings and goings and concerns were seen through the eyes of Laura Timmins, played by actress Olivia Hallinan, who, when the story began, moved from Lark Rise to the wealthier Candleford to begin a new life working for her mother's cousin Dorcas (Julia Sawalha) at the local post office.

Above: (right) Beautiful Chavenage, one of the main locations for *Lark Rise to Candleford*, *(right)* Dawn French with some young friends at Chavenage, one of the main locations for Lark Rise to Candleford, *(below)* Olivia Grant, who plays Lady Adelaide Midwinter, pictured during a break in filming.

Although set in Oxfordshire, *Lark Rise* (which also starred Dawn French in series one, two and four and Claudie Blakley), was actually filmed in and around Gloucestershire and Wiltshire, both at specially built studios and more prominently, at the stunning Chavenage House which played Sir Timothy Midwinter's home Candleford Manor.

Both interiors and exteriors of the Manor were shot extensively at Chavenage which is just outside the market town of Tetbury, taking full advantage of its beautiful gardens outside and its oak-floored and exquisitely decorated rooms inside, which are steeped in history.

These days the property is very much a family home, even though it is open to the public on a part-time basis and incidentally, is a perfect wedding venue. *Lark Rise to Candleford* wasn't the first time Chavenage was used as a film location – an episode of ITV's Poirot was shot there as was part of the 2008 BBC series *Bonekickers* and an episode of *Casualty*.

Fans of Lark Rise to Candleford will recognise many of the rooms used if they visit Chavenage such as the panelled Oak Room, which doubled up as Lady Adelaide's drawing room, the Ante Room, which served as Sir Timothy's office, and the Ballroom which was the dining room in the series. The Great Hall was also frequently on display as the hall at Candleford Manor and where characters were often seen passing through to the outside.

Most of the village scenes were shot at a Grade II listed farm at Box, five miles east of Bath, where a temporary village was specially created. Nearby Neston Park in Corsham, with its beautiful historical buildings, was also used as a backdrop for much of the series with many scenes shot on location in a farmyard. In addition, more than a dozen sets were built inside a vast warehouse in Yate, 12 miles north east of Bristol, for other village and town interior scenes.

For further details about Chavenage House telephone 01666 502329 or go to www.chavenage.com

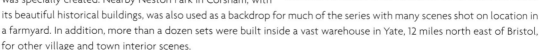

Sat nav references:

Chavenage House (GL8 8XP)
Neston Park (SN13 9TG)

Mistresses
Bristol

The tangled love lives of four 30-something modern women, all glamorous and successful in their own right, made Ecosse Films' drama for the BBC, *Mistresses*, unmissable week-night television when it was first screened in January 2008. Sadly, for many viewers, the show starring Sarah Parish, Sharon Small, Orla Brady, Shelley Conn and Joanna Lumley in the final series, was axed after season three in August 2010.

While the glossy drama could have been filmed anywhere, it was actually the more glamorous locations of Bristol that were selected and helped to give *Mistresses* a sophisticated feel. Bristol University doubled up as a restaurant in one episode and the General Medical Council in another, filming taking place after students left in the summer of 2007. The big finale sequence in series one took place in At Bristol, a hands-on science tourist attraction at trendy Millennium Square in the centre of the city. Real restaurants and hotels used in *Mistresses* included Bordeaux Quay on Canons Road, The Olive Shed at Princes Wharf and The Riverstation Restaurant (www.riverstation.co.uk). Other places of interest featured include the historic Blaise Castle Estate which boasts a small gothic castle dating back to the 18th Century called the Folly. The Folly is now a ruin and is open to the public on certain days during the summer only. For more information contact the Estate Office on 0117 353 2268.

Sat nav references:

Blaise Castle Estate (BS10 7QS)
Bordeaux Quay (BS1 5LL)
Olive Shed at Princes Wharf (BS1 4RN)

The Onedin Line
Dartmouth

Anyone who visited the pretty town of Dartmouth in Devon during certain periods of the 1970s must have thought they had walked through a time tunnel. For the clock was turned back on much of the town and surrounding areas while the BBC filmed its popular period drama *The Onedin Line*. The drama, which was set in the 1860s, followed the life of James Onedin, played by Peter Gilmore, as he ran his shipping line. Historic Bayard's Cove, which includes the Old Customs House and The Dartmouth Arms, was featured in several episodes. Nearby Bayard's Cove Fort was used for a Middle Eastern market scene as was the outside of the George and Dragon in Mayors Avenue and a scene supposedly in China was filmed in Avenue Gardens.

Above: Bayard's Cove in Dartmouth, a key location for *The Onedin Line*.

Sat nav references:

The Dartmouth Arms (TQ6 9AN)
George and Dragon (TQ6 9NG)
Maltster's Arms (TQ9 7EQ)

One Foot in the Grave
Christchurch

There were probably real cries of "I don't believe it!" in sleepy Tresillian Way, a small street in the village of Walkford near Christchurch in Dorset during the 1990s. For, as the real life setting for David Renwick's hit comedy series *One Foot in the Grave*, some

Above: (left) **Tresillian Way, Walkford** *(centre)* **tributes to Victor** *(right)* **Victor and Margaret.**

very strange things happened. Like 263 garden gnomes being delivered to the front lawn of poor old Victor Meldrew or an ancient Citroen being dumped in his skip. Life for Victor (Richard Wilson) was rather testing a lot of the time and that in turn didn't make things very easy for his long-suffering wife Margaret. The series ran from 1990 until 2000 and when Victor finally ended up in a grave after falling victim to a hit and run driver, fans made sure he wasn't forgotten. In fact floral tributes were laid near a railway bridge at Shawford near Winchester near to the spot where Victor met his end.

Only Fools and Horses
Bristol

It's no real wonder that the long arm of the law has never quite managed to catch up with dodgy dealing Del Boy Trotter. For if the boys in blue have been looking for Del in his manor of Peckham they've been looking in the wrong place. The late, great John Sullivan's brilliant *Only Fools And Horses* – which starred David Jason as wheeler-dealer Del Boy Trotter and Nicholas Lyndhurst as his dopey brother Rodney – became increasingly rarely shot in London - and has never actually been shot in Peckham. Debuting in 1981, it used to be filmed in and around the capital until it became too popular on screen and the crowds who gathered to watch filming grew too large. "Filming in London was a pain in the neck and we used to lose a lot of filming," said Ray Butt, the show's first producer. "I remember filming in Chapel Street in London and the crowds used to come round but they wouldn't be quiet and usually we'd have to stop during school breaks. It just became impossible to work."

Originally lots of London locations were used including Hammersmith cemetery, where Grandad's funeral took place, in *Strained Relations*, The Alma pub at the corner of Chapel Market and Baron Street in Islington which was seen in *It Never Rains* and *Diamonds Are For Heather* and Hanwell Community Centre Westcott Crescent, London, which was in *Cash and Curry*. Witley Gardens, Southall Green, was the street in *Ashes to Ashes*, where Trigger's grandfather's urn was sucked up by a passing road sweeper lorry and Ravenscourt Park in Hammersmith featured in the episode *As One Door Closes*.

Outside London, Butser Hill, near Petersfield, Hampshire was used for the hang gliding scene in *Tea For Three* and the Duke of Malebury's stately home in *A Royal Flush* was Clarendon Park, Wiltshire, but it isn't open to the public.

The series began to be filmed all around the country and there was a Nag's Head in Hull, Ipswich, Brighton, London and Bristol and a Peckham-style street market in Hull, Ipswich, Bristol and Salisbury. As Ray Butt said: "You can set up a street market anywhere. All you need is a long run of walls and then put some stalls out." Bristol became the most regularly used setting for the show.

"Architecturally it had everything we needed in terms of pubs, houses and a market and most importantly we found the right block of flats," said producer Gareth Gwenlan. So instead of Harlech Tower, Park Road East, Acton, London, which was the original setting, Whitemead House in Duckmoor Road, Bristol became Nelson Mandela House for the duration of filming and residents got used to seeing Del's dodgy yellow three-wheeler parked nearby.

From then on, many parts of Bristol were used for filming the show including: *In Dates*, Bristol North Baths, Gloucester Road, which was the police station, 46 Old Market Street, which was the dating

Above: (top) David Jason and Nicholas Lyndhurst share a joke during the filming of Only Fools and Horses, *(middle)* David Jason and Nicholas Lyndhurst take a break while filming Only Fools and Horses outside, *(bottom)* Whitemead House.

Above: **Del and Rodney do a runner.**

agency, and The White Horse, West Street, Bedminster, which was the Nag's Head. 187 Gloucester Road, now Planet Pizza, was where Trigger took a date and Shellard Road in Filton was where Rodney jumped a red light while trying to impress nervous Nerys. London also features briefly - the Trotter van flying over a bridge was shot at Talbot Road, Isleworth and Del and Raquel met under the clock at Waterloo Station. The Old Granary, Charlotte Street, appeared in *Yuppy Love*, where it served as the exterior location of the basement wine bar where Del famously fell over and also played a casino in *Fatal Extraction*, is now a Loch Fyne restaurant. Across the road at 46-48 Charles Fox House was the location of Rodney's adult education class. The Parkside Night Club, Bath Road, 10-16 York Street (which was used as Alan Parry's business), flats at Guild Court, Redcliffe Back and the Boardwalk Shopping Centre were all used in *Rodney Come Home*. Henry Africas Hothouse, Whiteladies Road and Shoots floating restaurant were both used for *The Chance of a Lunchtime* and Raquel's audition in *Stage Fright* took place at the Courage Social Club in Willway Road.

The Conservatory Bar at Arnos Manor Hotel on Bath Road in Bristol was used in *Danger UXD* in the scene where Rodney took Cassandra to dinner. The hotel was also the venue for disco scenes in *Yuppy Love* and *Rodney Come Home*. The rear of Arnos Manor Hotel in Bath Road was used in *Chain Gang* as the One Eleven Club. Lockside Cafe on Brunel Lock Road, Bristol was the location for Sid's Cafe in the 1993 Christmas Special *Fatal Extraction* and the 1996 episodes Heroes and *Villains and Modern Men*. Back then it was a greasy spoon, but now, according to its website (www.lockside.net) it is a 'polished spoon.' A car showroom on Marsh Road was the location for Boycie's car showroom in *Time on our Hands* and Bristol City's car park at Ashton Gate was used as a market in *Fatal Extraction, Heroes and Villains* and *Strangers on the Shore*. But Bristol didn't have a monopoly on filming. For example, the former Bembom Brothers' funfair at Margate (now called Dreamland), the Roman Galley pub in Thanet Way, Canterbury (which has now been converted into flats called Galley View) and the forecourt of Margate railway station were all used for the episode *The Jolly Boys' Outing* and Tandoori Nights, King Street, London appeared in Chain Gang. It was also back to London for scenes of Del and Rodney searching for Albert in *He Ain't Heavy, He's My Uncle* and the following places were used: Tower Bridge, HMS Belfast, Portobello Green, Acklam Road East, Malton Road and Portobello Road Market. The airport used in *The Sky's The Limit* was Stansted.

The hilarious scene when Raquel gave birth to Damian Trotter was supposed to be in Peckham but was actually filmed at the maternity wing of Hillingdon Hospital in Uxbridge in the episode *Three Men, a Woman and a Baby*. The scenes of Damian's christening in *Miami Twice: The American Dream* were actually filmed at two different churches. The interior scenes were filmed at St John's Church in Ladbroke Grove and the outside shots were done at St John's Church in Kentish Town. The Nag's Head used for the 1992 Christmas Special *Mother Nature's Son* was the White Admiral Pub at Lower Bevendean in Brighton (sadly now demolished with flats built on the site) not far from the allotments in Natal Road which were used as Grandad's old allotment in Peckham.

The area in front of Whitemead House, Bristol, was used for the riot scene in *Fatal Extraction*. It was back to Bristol for the famous Batman and Robin scene in *Heroes and Villains* which was filmed at the shopping centre at The Horsefair in Broadmead and Rodney chased a yob past shops in Oxford Street and also down Nottingham Street and Hill Avenue in the same episode. The Harrison watch was found at Del's garage, a stone's throw from Whitemead House and when the Trotters sold it in *Time on Our Hands*, the auction scenes were filmed at Sotheby's, 34-35 New Bond Street, London. Marine Parade, Woodland Road, and the Dragon Kiss restaurant in Regent Street, Weston-Super-Mare all appeared in *If They Could See Us Now* and if you fancy a trip abroad, Del and Rodney took a ferry from Portsmouth to represent Albert at a ceremony in France, scenes for which were filmed in Gatteville-le-Phare. Finally, in the last episode *Sleepless in Peckham*, Greenbank Cemetery in Greenbank Road, Bristol was used for a moving scene where Rodney and Del visited their Mum's grave. The 2014 *Sport Relief* sketch was filmed on the former *Family Affairs* set at Wimbledon Studios.

Sat nav references:

The Alma Pub (N1 9EX)
Arnos Manor Hotel (BS4 3HQ)
Dragon Kiss restaurant (BS23 1SQ)
Greenbank Cemetery (BS5 6HL)
Henry Africas Hot House (BS8 2LY)
Hillingdon Hospital (UB8 3NN)
Loch Fyne restaurant (BS1 4HQ)
Lockside Cafe (BS1 6XS)
Planet Pizza (BS7 8BG)
Sotheby's (W1A 2AA)
Tandoori Nights (W6 9NH)

Persuasion
Bath

Beautiful and historical Bath featured heavily in ITV's stunning adaptation of Jane Austen's *Persuasion* which was filmed in 2006 and screened the following year to critical acclaim. It's a city close to Jane Austen's heart as she lived there in the early 1800s and chose it as the setting for both *Northanger Abbey* and *Persuasion*. This version starred Rupert Penry-Jones as Captain Wentworth and Sally Hawkins as Anne Elliot, an 'old maid' of 27 living a quiet life with her noble family in their country manor home, Kellynch Hall until events forced a change on the whole family, particularly Anne.

Above: Bath Street in Bath - used for a market scene in ITV's 2006 version of *Persuasion*. *Below*: Rupert Penry-Jones and Sally Hawkins pictured during a break in the filming of *Persuasion*.

As much of *Persuasion* as possible was filmed in Bath but there were a few locations outside the city which were also used, including beach scenes at Lyme Regis in Dorset and at Golden Cap, five miles east of Lyme Regis. Stunning Sheldon Manor (www.sheldonmanor.co.uk) in Chippenham doubled as Uppercross Hall where Anne decamped after her family were forced to leave Kellynch. The Coaching Inn which, supposedly at Lyme Regis, was actually shot at Great Chalfield Manor, a National Trust property near Melksham in Wiltshire.

The interior of Camden Place, the Bath property the Elliott family headed to after leasing out Kellynch, was actually Neston Park in Corsham and the exterior was Number One Royal Crescent in the centre of Bath. The National Trust-owned Assembly Rooms in Bennett Street were used to stage a concert during which Captain Wentworth saw Anne and left. Bennett Street itself was also used as the address of Mrs Smith and Westgate Buildings. It also doubled as Queens Square, which itself was too small to close down for filming purposes. Royal Crescent doubled as Camden Place to where Anne's father and sister moved when they left Kellynch and the romantic final scene where Anne and Wentworth kissed at the end of Persuasion was also shot there.

The beautiful Botanical Gardens in Royal Victoria Park became the exterior of Queens Square and nearby Western Road was closed during shooting to minimise noise. The very narrow cobbled Queen Street was used on another day for a scene in which Wentworth was searching for Anne. He looked in an art shop window for which a shop was specially dressed. The final day of filming took place at Green Park where Anne and Wentworth finally admitted their feelings to each other. Grand Parade was also used for one of these closing scenes, along with Bath Street.

The 1995 version of *Persuasion* was arguably the BBC's finest adaptation of a Jane Austen novel by virtue of Director Roger Michell's deliberately dowdy costumes and settings, making it altogether less glossy than other Austen dramatisations. Much was filmed in Bath with both the Assembly Rooms and Pump Room being used for some scenes including a concert. The nearby Abbey Churchyard also featured as did 13 Old Bond Street, now a Starbucks coffee shop, which played a teashop. Outside Bath Sheldon Manor at Chippenham, the surviving manor house of a long gone Medieval village, also appeared in this version doubling as The Musgroves' home. Barnsley House at Barnsley near Cirencester in Gloucestershire played Kellynch Hall.

Sat nav references:

Assembly Rooms (BA1 2QH)
Barnsley House (GL7 5EE),
Great Chalfield Manor (SN12 8NH)
Neston Park in Corsham (SN13 9TG)
Number One Royal Crescent (BA1 2LR)
Sheldon Manor (SN14 0RG)

Above: Stunning St Mawes Castle in Falmouth, doubled as a French fort in *Poldark*.

Poldark
Cornwall

Cornwall was the setting for *Poldark*, the BBC's swashbuckling saga about heroic war veteran Ross Poldark, played by Robin Ellis. Set in the 18th Century, the series was a huge hit with viewers both in Britain and around the world, who revelled in the stories of tin mining, smuggling and skulduggery. Now, nearly 40 years on (*Poldark* ran between 1975 and 1977), the BBC has announced it will be making a new six-part series of *Poldark*, once again returning to film in Cornwall.

In the '70s episodes, Ross and his wife Demelza, played by Angharad Rees lived at Nampara, which is actually a stone farmhouse, Botallack Manor. Other scenes at Nampara were filmed at nearby Pendeen Manor. Ross's cousin Francis and his wife Elizabeth lived at Trenwith. In the first series Trenwith was played by Tudor Godolphin House at Godolphin Cross. Godolphin, which is now owned by the National Trust, was used when Trenwith was attacked by miners and scenes where Ross Poldark first met Demelza at the Redruth Fair were filmed in the grounds.

Dr Dwight Enys' home in the series was actually Doyden Castle, a gothic folly built in the 19th Century. The folly, at Port Quin in north Cornwall, is high up on the cliffs and has spectacular views. It can be rented from the National Trust. Not far from Port Quin, at Trebetherick, is Enodoc Church which was used for the wedding of Francis and Elizabeth. Another church, Towednack, was used for Francis' father's funeral. Lots of filming took place on the north coast from Botallack in the far west to the River Camel where Padstow stands, in the Penzance area, Prussia Cove, and on the south coast at Charlestown, which was also used for the 1998 ITV drama *Frenchman's Creek*. Cornwall also doubled for France with part of the Fowey estuary near Lerryn Creek playing a landing point for Ross and his friends in their bid to free Dr Enys from French prison Fort Baton. St Mawes Castle, an English Heritage property at the entrance to Falmouth, played the fort. See www.english-heritage.org.uk for further details.

Sat nav references:

Botallack Manor (TR19 7QG)
Enodoc Church (PL27 6SA)
Pendeen Manor (TR19 7ED)
St Mawes Castle (TR2 5DE)
Tudor Godolphin House (TR13 9RE)

Sense and Sensibility
Bideford

Anyone familiar with the stunning coastal walkway between Hartland Quay and Hartland Point which is to be found on the Hartland Abbey Estate near Bideford, north Devon may well have recognised it while watching the BBC's superb adaptation of Jane Austen's *Sense and Sensibility*. It was here that much of the three-part serialisation starring such names as David Morrissey and Janet McTeer was filmed during an often wet May 2007. The Estate, which has been classified as an area of

Above: Loseley House, a key location for *Sense and Sensibility*.

outstanding natural beauty, is owned by Sir Hugh and Lady Angela Stucley. Tucked away in a sheltered valley is Blackpool Mill Cottage which was also heavily featured in the drama as Barton Cottage.

It was to here that the Dashwood Family – sisters Elinor (Hattie Morahan) and Marianne (Charity Wakefield) - decamped upon the death of their father along with their widowed mother (McTeer) and began to build themselves a new life. But the cottage seen in the drama looked somewhat different to the actual building used, thanks to the skills of the BBC's set designers.

The BBC also obtained the family's permission to paint the cottage and then returned it to its natural state once filming was over. If you fancy staying at Blackpool Mill cottage, it is available for rent for up to eight people. See www.hartlandabbey.com for details. In some scenes part of the grounds of the Abbey were used as the carriageway for other stately homes the BBC filmed at. These include Dorney Court in Windsor, Berkshire which served as the grand home of Sir John Middleton (played by Mark Williams). It was here that a lavish dinner party scene took place as did the rehearsal for a ball the Dashwood sisters attended. Privately owned, it is a Grade I listed building of outstanding historical interest. See www.dorneycourt.co.uk for further details.

Above: Picturesque Blackpool Mill Cottage used as Barton Cottage in *Sense and Sensibility*.

The sumptuous 17th Century Ham House on the banks of the River Thames at Ham, Richmond-Upon-Thames doubled up as Cleveland. The house, which belongs to the National Trust, has stunning formal gardens as well as gorgeous interiors and original collections. The spectacular Dyrham House, a William and Mary mansion set in a deer park, also belonging to the Trust was used to shoot many of the garden scenes. The location could also be glimpsed in the movie *Remains of the Day* shot in 1993. Finally, the splendid library at historic Loseley Park just outside Guildford, Surrey played Colonel Brandon's library. The front entrance of Loseley was also used in *Sense and Sensibility* for the scenes in which Colonel Brandon and his guests, including the Dashwoods, gathered in preparation for his picnic which didn't happen as he was called away on urgent business. The House also doubled as the exterior of Sir John's home which, of course, was set in Devon in the story, while its impressive Oak Room was used in the series to nurse a sick Marianne after her walk in the rain. See www.loseley-park.com for more information.

Sat nav references:

Blackpool Mill Cottage (EX39 6DT)
Dorney Court (SL4 6QP)
Dyrham House (SN14 8ER)
Ham House (TW10 7RS)
Hartland Abbey Estate (EX39 6DT)
Loseley Park (GU3 1HS)

Skins
Bristol

Teen drama *Skins* began airing on E4 then Channel 4 in 2007 and proved to be a huge hit, particularly with youngsters who could identify with its modern-day issues such as relationship angst, infidelity, drugs and pressures of school. It finally bowed out in July 2013 after seven series.

Focusing on a group of Bristol teenagers, the city itself featured heavily throughout most episodes. A number of Bristol landmarks were easily recognisable such as Bristol Cathedral which was shown in the opening credits of series one and the Pur Down BT transmission tower situated to the right of the M32 as you enter Bristol, with wonderful views over the city in the opening credits of series two. The unit base for *Skins* was in a large warehouse in Fishponds, north Bristol where specially-constructed sets were used for house and club interiors. For exteriors, Brandon Hill was used a fair amount, one of the city's oldest public parks, gifted to the council in 1147 by the Earl of Gloucester and boasting spectacular views across Bristol. For details of opening times contact Bristol Parks on 0117 922 3719.

Other parks and council-owned estates around Bristol used for filming included The Kings Weston Estate, Oldbury Court Estate, Ashton Court Estate and Queens Square. For series one many college scenes were shot at The John Cabot Academy, an independent school in Kingswood, north east Bristol. For series two the production team decided to recreate the headmaster's office and a classroom on a studio set and so used the Academy a lot less.

About 200 yards from Brandon Hill is College Green (picture on opposite page) which is at the bottom of Park Street, outside the council offices. It is here that the teens in Skins often congregated after class and was a regular feature. On screen it was supposedly right outside the college when actually it was filmed in a totally different location. Other places of interest to visitors are Thekla which is a cool boat that sits on the side of Bristol Harbour and where the characters had a big party in series three. Go to www.theklabristol.co.uk for more details. Nightclubs used in Skins included Lakota, La Rocca and The Croft which are popular and well-known. The main Bristol University building often doubled up for several different venues in early seasons of *Skins* while the once-derelict Pro-Cathedral was used as the venue for a huge 'secret party' in season two which was filmed exclusively for the internet and to which 500 fans of the show were invited. The building has since been redeveloped.

Sat nav references:

Ashton Court Estate (BS41 9DW)
Brandon Hill (BS1 5RR)
Bristol Cathedral (BS1 5TJ)
The Croft (BS1 3RW)
John Cabot Academy (BS15 8BD)
The Kings Weston Estate (BS11 0UR)
Lakota (BS2 8QN)
La Rocca (BS8 1EY)
Oldbury Court Estate (BS16 2QX)

To the Manor Born
Cricket St Thomas

The BBC had a winner on its hands in 1979 with its comedy series *To the Manor Born*. The show starred Penelope Keith as frightfully posh Audrey Fforbes-Hamilton who, stung by death duties, was forced to sell her stately home, Grantleigh Manor, and live in the estate's tiny lodge, taking her butler Brabinger and her beagle Benjie with her.

Grantleigh Manor was bought by self-made millionaire grocer Richard De Vere who, certainly in the eyes of Mrs Fforbes-Hamilton, didn't come from the right kind of background necessary to live in such a place. But he obviously grew on her, as they married at the end of the series and were still together in a special episode shown at Christmas 2007.

The series was filmed on the elegant Cricket St Thomas estate, near Chard in Somerset. Cricket House naturally played Grantleigh Manor and the estate's lodge played Mrs Fforbes-Hamilton's modest residence. The estate was bought in 1998 by Warner Leisure Hotels and the house, which was built in 1785 and is Grade II listed, has been turned into a resort hotel offering four-star accommodation. For details of how to book accommodation at Cricket St Thomas see www.warnerleisurehotels.co.uk

Above: (left) Filming To the Manor Born at night, *(centre)* Cricket St Thomas, alias Grantleigh Manor, *(right)* the famous clapperboard. *Top right:* Penelope Keith and Peter Bowles filming the 2007 Christmas special.

Sat nav references:

Cricket St Thomas estate (TA20 4DD)

Wild West

Filmed at Portloe, on the south Cornwall coast, which doubled as fictional St Gweep, Simon Nye's comedy, which ran from 2002 to 2004, starred Dawn French as lesbian Mary Trewednack who ran a shop with her partner Angela.

Wycliffe
Cornwall

Above: **Stunning Caerhays beach in Cornwall.** *Below:* Jack Shepherd as Charles Wycliffe

In terms of stunning locations, the ITV detective drama *Wycliffe* was the best television advertisement for the beautiful county of Cornwall since *Poldark* was filmed by the BBC back in the 70s. Jack Shepherd starred as likeable Cornish sleuth Detective Superintendent Charles Wycliffe alongside his faithful team of Jimmy Yuill and Helen Masters as Detective Inspectors Doug Kersey and Lucy Lane.

Together they solved all manner of baffling cases during the show's five series which ran from a pilot episode in 1993 until 1998. The production base was Truro but locations all over Cornwall from quiet farmhouses and pretty fishing villages to cliffs buffeted by raging seas and upmarket houses were used in the filming of the show.

The dramatic scene in the opening episode when a man walking his dog was gunned down was filmed at Caerhays beach below Caerhays Castle. In another episode a burning wheel was pushed off a stunning peak, actually the National Trust's Pentire Point, a beauty spot much loved by walkers. The wild-west theme park featured in the episode *The Scapegoat* was actually Frontier City near St Columb Major and the whole village of St Ewe was taken over by the film crew for the episode *The Last Rites*.

Other key scenes were filmed at Porthleven, Redruth, Portreath, Goonhilly Down (the BT communications centre), Carharrach and Kennach Sands. The shot of an exploding fishing boat in the episode *The Pea Green Boat* was filmed off Godrevy Point near Hayle and a car going off a cliff in the same episode was filmed at Porthowan.

Sat nav references:

Caerhays Castle (PL26 6LY)

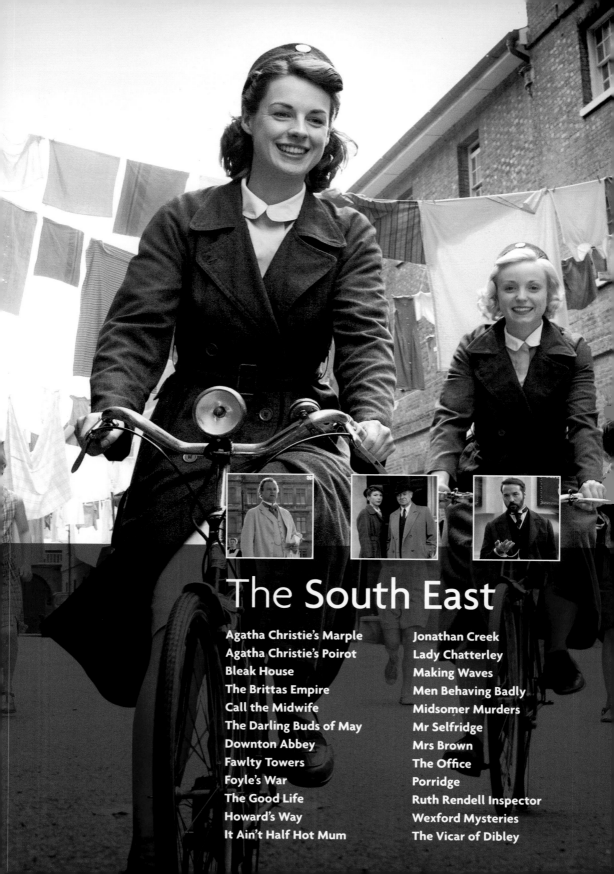

The South East

Agatha Christie's Marple
Agatha Christie's Poirot
Bleak House
The Brittas Empire
Call the Midwife
The Darling Buds of May
Downton Abbey
Fawlty Towers
Foyle's War
The Good Life
Howard's Way
It Ain't Half Hot Mum

Jonathan Creek
Lady Chatterley
Making Waves
Men Behaving Badly
Midsomer Murders
Mr Selfridge
Mrs Brown
The Office
Porridge
Ruth Rendell Inspector
Wexford Mysteries
The Vicar of Dibley

Agatha Christie's Marple
Chilterns

This hugely successful ITV drama series began screening in 2004. Along with *Agatha Christie's Poirot,* it was shot in a wealth of locations across the Chilterns and sometimes beyond. Every episode used a number of locations often spread miles apart, yet as in *Poirot*, viewers were led to believe every scene had been shot in just one place.

Above: Holly Willoughby, who appeared in a cameo role in *The Pale Horse* chats to super sleuth Miss Marple (Julia McKenzie) during a break from filming episode *The Pale Horse. Below:* Knebworth House, which is used regularly for filming.

For instance, a number of separate houses were used to serve as Rutherford Hall in the 2004 film *4.50 from Paddington*, including Highclere Castle in Hampshire (see *Downton Abbey* section), Loseley Park in Guildford and Knebworth House in Stevenage, Hertfordshire. Eltham Palace in Court Road, Eltham served as Noel Coward's house while far further afield in Leicestershire, Rothley Station was Paddington Station in London.

The role of Miss Marple has been played on film and television by a range of actresses including notably Margaret Rutherford, Gracie Fields and Angela Lansbury and, of course, Joan Hickson who appeared in a long-running series of BBC films. For the most recent ITV series of films, actress Geraldine McEwan first undertook the title role with actress Julia McKenzie replacing her in 2009.

Many of the locations used to shoot the *Marple* films have popped up in other shows as they are popular with production companies, usually for their convenience and beauty. For example, the picturesque village of Turville in Buckinghamshire was often used to shoot *Marple* scenes and can also be spotted in episodes of *Midsomer Murders*, *Lewis* and of course *The Vicar of Dibley* to name but a few.

The Secret of Chimneys, which was screened at Christmas 2010, was shot in a number of locations including Hatfield House and once again at Knebworth House. Hatfield House, a magnificent Jacobean estate in Hatfield, Hertfordshire, was used to shoot the exterior of family house Chimneys. The house is one of the so-called Treasure Houses of England, of which there are only ten and is the home of the 7th Marquess of Salisbury. Elizabeth I spent much of her childhood here and indeed learnt of her accession to the throne while staying there. See www.hatfield-house.co.uk for more details.

Chimney's interiors were filmed mainly at the superb Knebworth House in nearby Stevenage which has been home to the Lytton family since 1490. The imposing property is in a Tudor Gothic style and well worth a visit. It is open to the public who particularly love its spectacular gardens. It is also popular with film production companies with movies including parts of *The King's Speech* and *Harry Potter and the Goblet of Fire* being shot there in recent years. See www.knebworthhouse.com for more details.

Sat nav references:

Dorney Court (SL4 6QP)
Eltham Palace (SE9 5QE)
Hatfield House (AL9 5NQ)
Highclere Castle (RG20 9RN)
Knebworth House (SG3 6PY)
Lincolns Inn (WC2A 3TL)
Loseley Park (GU3 1HS)
Rothley Station (LE7 7LD)

Other scenes in the film were shot in various locations including Langley Park House, an 18th Century Grade II listed property built as a hunting lodge for the 3rd Duke of Marlborough. The basement doubled up as a series of tunnels which on screen were part of Chimneys.

The Pale Horse episode was shot at Tudor manor house Dorney Court (which has also popped up in *Midsomer Murders* and was used in the 2009 BBC version of *The Day of the Triffids*), Lincolns Inn and some of Temple, London. See www.dorneycourt.co.uk

The first episode of Marple to be screened in 2013 was *A Caribbean Mystery* with

Cape Town in South Africa doubling as the island of St Honore. Next to be broadcast was *Greenshaw's Folly*, shot at a range of locations including Shirburn Castle in Oxfordshire, Knebworth House, Rotherfield Park and St Joseph's College in Mill Hill. *Endless Night*, the final episode for 2013, was filmed in nearly a dozen locations including Chinnor Quarry, Oxfordshire, West Wycombe House, West Wycombe, Cliveden House in Taplow, Fawley Court in Henley-on-Thames, The Homewood, Esher, the village of Dorchester-on-Thames, Oxfordshire, Longcross Manor in Surrey and the Duke of York Steps, London.

Agatha Christie's Poirot
Chilterns

This hugely successful detective drama began on ITV in 1989 and the final film Curtain was completed in 2013. Actor David Suchet played the role of Belgian sleuth Hercule Poirot in all 70 films and it was always his ambition to do all of Agatha Christie's Poirot stories. Like *Agatha Christie's Marple*, the locations used may have been nowhere near each other, yet we the viewers were led to believe the whole story was shot in the same place.

The picturesque village of Hambleden between Marlow in Buckinghamshire and Henley-on-Thames featured heavily in *Mrs McGinty's Dead* which was screened in 2008, and indeed popped up in various *Poirots* over the years. Tucked in the foothills of the Chilterns, the village is an idyllic cluster of flint cottages, complete with a pub, church and village square. It could have been designed for a drama such as *Poirot*. In the story Hambleden doubled up as the village of Broadhinny where Poirot was called in to investigate the murder of a charwoman.

Some of the early *Poirots* were shot far and wide while more latterly, reduced budgets meant production crews tended to travel overnight for no more than two days per film. Therefore every effort was made to keep filming locations as close to each other as possible, although this was not always the case. For example, locations for the 2007 episode *Mrs McGinty's Dead* included parts of Dover in Kent, West Wycombe Park in Buckinghamshire (always a popular filming choice) and the Bluebell Railway in East Sussex (www.bluebell-railway.co.uk) which often crops up in TV productions as it is close to London and comes complete with period stations and rolling stock. It was also used for a 1999 ITV version of *The Railway Children*.

A particularly famous *Agatha Christie's Poirot* story is *Murder on the Orient Express* with millions tuning in to ITV1's version when it was screened in December 2010. However, despite appearances the film wasn't

Above: David Suchet as *Poirot* filming *Murder on the Orient Express* on location. *Below:* Behind the scenes on *Murder on the Orient Express* members of the crew operate a snow machine to create a snowdrift in Black Park.

shot anywhere near the real train which may surprise fans as it appeared beautifully authentic on screen. In fact the carriages used for filming were specially created at Pinewood Studios. The snowdrift scenes where all the passengers (and suspects) found themselves stranded were recreated close to the studios in woods in Black Park. This time, the carriages used were real and 'borrowed' from the Nene Valley Railway, Peterborough. "We made the drifts using sandbags and then powered up the snow machines to create the look we wanted," explained Chris White the location manager on the shoot.

Much of this particular film was also shot on location in Malta. Other locations worth pointing out that featured in other *Poirots* include Dover Castle for *The Clocks*, where its tunnels were the perfect backdrop for secret liaisons between officers in the intelligence service; Chenies Manor, Buckinghamshire (www.cheniesmanorhouse.co.uk) for *Hallowe'en Party*; Cambridge University for *The Case of the Missing Will*; Somerset; Brighton and of course abroad. The interior of Poirot's apartment was a specially constructed set at Pinewood Studios, while the exterior used was Florin Court, an art deco block of flats in Charterhouse Square, London.

The 2013 story *Elephants Can Remember* was filmed at locations including Greys Court, a National Trust property in Henley-on-Thames, Netherwylde Equestrian in Hertfordshire, the Park Lane Hotel and both Shepperton and Pinewood Studios. Locations for *The Big Four* included Longcross Manor House, Nuffield Place, Kensal Green Cemetery and the Hackney Empire and for *The Labours of Hercules*, Brocket Hall (www.brocket-hall.co.uk) and RAF Halton House. *Dead Man's Folly* locations included High Canons in Borehamwood, the Wormsley Estate, the National Trust's Hughenden Manor and Agatha Christie's real holiday home, Greenway House, in Devon, which is also a National Trust property. Scenes for the final episode, *Curtain*, were filmed in Oxford, Surrey and at Pinewood Studios.

Sat nav references:

Bluebell Railway (TN22 3QL)
Cambridge University (CB2 1TN)
Charterhouse Square (EC1M 6EA)
Chenies Manor (WD3 6ER)
Dover Castle (CT16 1HU)
Freemasons Hall (WC2B 5AZ)
Royal Courts of Justice (WC2A 2LL)

Above: **Balls Park, Hertford.**
Below: **Caddy Jellyby (Nathalie Press) embraces her mother Mrs Jellyby (Liza Tarbuck) in a scene from** *Bleak House.*

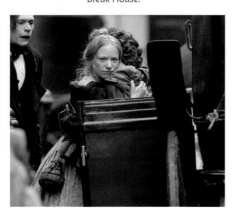

Bleak House
Hertford

Even audiences who had never thought Charles Dickens could be interesting were captivated by the BBC's adaptation of his classic *Bleak House* which was screened in the autumn of 2005. Penned by Andrew Davies and produced by Nigel Stafford-Clark, what made *Bleak House* so watchable was its large and impressive cast of household names. The American actress Gillian Anderson of *The X-Files* was first to jump aboard followed by such stars as Pauline Collins, Alun Armstrong, Denis Lawson and Charles Dance, to name but a few.

With a huge cast and an ambitious number of hours to shoot, filming locations were more important than ever. It was clear it would be both time and cost-effective not to move around too much if possible and so it was decided that just one large house with the necessary historical features should be used to film various different locations, as opposed to either building a set from scratch or moving from one venue to another.

Balls Park, a Grade I listed building just outside Hertford proved to be the ideal building for it had everything required to make it a practical first choice. "It even had a room we were able to use as Chancery which is at the heart of Bleak House and around which all the various stories revolve," explained Nigel Stafford-Clark. So it was here that the likes of the interior of Bleak House itself, Tulkinghorn's offices and even the garrets above Krook's shop which were created in the eaves, came to life so convincingly. The interior of the big court room, Lincoln's Inn Court, was also filmed at Balls Park.

The exterior of Balls Park doubled up as the exterior of Boythorn's house and the stunning 16th Century mansion Ingatestone Hall in Essex served as the exterior of Bleak House. Go to www.ingatestonehall.com for details. Charles Dickens himself lived in Kent for many years and is known to have strolled through the grounds of the very impressive Cobham Hall, a 12th Century manor house set in 150 acres of Grade II listed parkland. The BBC used the exterior of the very same Cobham Hall as the exterior of Lady Dedlock's home, Chesney Wold. It also served as the exterior of the Inns of Court. The interior of the Hall was also used for some scenes. Go to www.cobhamhall.com to learn more about the Hall's history and for public opening times.

Less than an hour from Balls Park, up the M1 motorway, the old farm yard of Luton Hoo was ingeniously transformed into the cobbled streets of London. This historic Grade I listed building is now a luxury five star hotel but half of the estate is still a working farm which proved perfect for the BBC's needs. Down town London was cleverly created by the BBC's art department by filming around and on top of the majority of the existing buildings on the Luton Hoo estate, while a lot of the interior of the farm buildings were turned into the ground floor of Krook's and Snagsby's shops.

Sat nav references:
Balls Park (SG1 8QE)
Cobham Hall (DA12 3BL)
Luton Hoo (LU1 3TQ)

Call the Midwife
Chatham

This family-friendly drama about midwives in the 1950s was a surprise hit with viewers when it first aired on BBC1 in 2012. Indeed *Call the Midwife* became one of the most popular shows in a decade, pulling in audiences of more than nine million viewers each Sunday evening, leaping up to 11.4 million when the Christmas special trounced its rivals in the festive day ratings battle. The second series screened in January 2013 proved equally popular, despite the often gloomy and unglamorous settings.

Starring Miranda Hart as plummy Chummy, Jenny Agutter as Sister Julienne and Jessica Raine as the naïve Jennifer Worth, on whose memoirs the show is based, the drama, produced by Neal Street Productions, centres on the poverty-stricken communities of Poplar in London's East End and the midwives, many of them nuns, on call to help them. The midwives are often seen cycling through cobbled streets and alleyways to visit their patients, many living in slum conditions.

Yet these narrow, quaint streets were actually shot on location miles from London at Chatham Historic Dockyard in Kent, described as "the finest example of a dockyard in the Age of Sail anywhere in the world." It has also proved to be a favoured filming location and used for such movies as *Les Miserables*, *Sherlock Holmes* and *The Golden Compass* and TV dramas including *Tipping the Velvet*, *Mr Selfridge* and

Above: **The cast of *Call The Midwife* at Nonnatus House**

Vanity Fair to name but a few.

For the purposes of filming *Call the Midwife*, the area was transported back to the 50s relatively easily with very little work done to the exteriors of the buildings to create the docks and the industrial areas. In the main, set dressing was used consisting of crates, barrels and tarpaulins. In series one, shipping containers were covered in material to represent large items on the dockside. The set was also covered with vehicles, often to disguise modern day trappings and while some of these were from the Historic Dockyard's own collection, the majority were hired through a specialist agency.

The setting was further enhanced by the use of the Historic Dockyard's own steam trains. These trains operate at special events and once a month on the internal railway within the dockyard. They were specially hired by the producers of *Call the Midwife* and appeared on several occasions.

Much of the drama occurs in residential areas and these were created at Chatham between the buildings which run parallel to the wharf and dressed with the washing lines that have become synonymous with the show. These industrial areas were transformed by the addition of false doorways leading into the residential tenement blocks that they represent on screen, while the use of a large number of supporting artistes brought these areas to life.

Other areas at the south of the dockyard have been used to represent the industrial

Above: Jessica Raine and Bryony Hannah filming in Chatham Dockyard.

areas around the docks and other residential properties, often appearing several times in different episodes but made to look different by the careful use of props and vehicles and different camera angles.

The first series was filmed in the summer of 2011 while series two and the Christmas special were shot in the summer of 2012. The Christmas special may have looked appropriately cold and snowy on screen, but this was thanks to careful filming and editing which ensured every seasonal flower and leafy tree was removed from each frame. Also, a paper-based fake snow effect was used which turned into a soggy mess when it was washed away!

Nigel Crisp of the Historic Dockyard said having the BBC cast and crew on site was a nothing but a pleasure. "It's a cliché to say everyone got on well and were very friendly but it's true!" he insisted. "We thoroughly enjoyed having them around and are looking forward to having them back for another series. From our point of view, the site is so large that filming has little impact on general visitors and brings with it an element of excitement and fun."

Chatham Historic Dockyard is now running *Call the Midwife* guided tours so fans of the show can visit all the areas they've seen on screen. Telephone 01634 823852 to pre-book or go to www.thedockyard.co.uk

The building which was used as Nonnatus House, where the midwives live, can be found in Mill Hill, North London. St Joseph's College is a beautiful disused Gothic seminary and was skilfully transformed by Oscar-nominated production designer Eve Stewart.

It was used for the kitchen, dining room, bedrooms, clinical room and as interiors for many of the guest characters' homes. In the spring of 2013 St Joseph's College was sold to developers with planning permission for 49 residential apartments so for the third series, which was screened in early 2014, filming switched to Longcross Studios in Chertsey, a former tank factory and MOD research facility which has previously been used for the filming of many television dramas including *Enid*, *Lewis*, *Echo Beach* and *Moving Wallpaper* along with scenes for films including *Skyfall*, *Wrath of the Titans* and *War Horse*.

The Manor House - a former Officers' Mess - was used as the New Nonnatus House and designer Eve Stewart also built a set near the house so exteriors were filmed there too. The Neal Street Productions team built new interior sets - including a community centre where antenatal clinics take place inside Building 99 at Longcross. The real-life Nonnatus House where Jennifer Worth lived was actually Saint Frideswide's Mission House in Lodore Street, Poplar. It closed in 1978 and the building has now been converted into flats.

Above: (top) Helen George (Trixie Franklin), Miranda Hart (Chummy), Jessica Raine (Jenny Lee) and Bryony Hannah (Cynthia Miller), *(middle)* St Joseph's College, Mill Hill, which played Nonnatus House, *(left)* Jessica Raine (Jenny Lee) Helen George (Trixie Franklin) and Bryony Hannah (Cynthia Miller) — and three young actors.

Sat nav references:

Chatham Historic Dockyard (ME4 4TE)
St Joseph's College (NW7 4JX)

The Darling Buds of May
Pluckley

The sleepy village of Pluckley in Kent had never expected the attention that it suddenly received in the summer of 1991. For the instant success of Yorkshire Television's *The Darling Buds of May*, starring the ever-popular David Jason as Pop Larkin, brought hordes of fans into the village, which is said to be one of the most haunted places in Britain.

The quaint 15th Century Black Horse pub played the Hare and Hounds in the series. "We still get people coming to the village because of *The Darling Buds of May*," said landlord Kevin Savidge. "And they also come here for the ghosts as we're one of the most haunted pubs in the country – and we've been on television quite a lot for that too."

Just across the road is the grocer's shop, which featured in the series, as did Pluckley butcher's shop next door. Nearby St Nicholas' Parish Church became a star attraction in the series when Mariette, played by Catherine Zeta Jones, married Charley (Philip Franks). It

Above: David Jason on location at Buss Farm, the main location for *The Darling Buds of May*.

was also used when Primrose Larkin (Abigail Rokison) was chasing the Reverend Candy, played by Tyler Butterworth.

Next door to the church is the house that played guide mistress Edith Pilchester's home and opposite the church is the small house, which played Orchard Cottage where the Brigadier, played by Moray Watson, lived. A few doors away is the local school which was used in the series as the village hall.

Above: (left) **David Jason as Pop Larkin** *(centre)* **The Black Horse pub, which doubled as The Hare and Hounds in the series** *(right)* **Pam Ferris, David Jason and Catherine Zeta Jones.**

A few miles away from Pluckley, on the road to Smarden, is Buss Farm, which played the Larkins' Home Farm. The Grade II main farmhouse was bought in 2012 by a businessman who plans on refurbishing the property. He has also submitted plans to renovate some of the outbuildings on the farm with a view to letting them out so visitors may soon be able to enjoy the *Darling Buds of May* experience. Some scenes in later episodes of the show, supposedly in Kent, were actually filmed hundreds of miles away in Yorkshire - to save time and money.

Sat nav references:

Black Horse pub (TN27 0QS)
St Nicholas' Parish Church (TN27 0QS)
Pluckley School (TN27 0QS)

Downton Abbey
Newbury

With its stellar cast including Hugh Bonneville, Dame Maggie Smith and Jim Carter, not to mention its creator and screenwriter, Gosford Park's Lord Julian Fellowes, it was perhaps inevitable ITV1's *Downton Abbey* would become an instant hit when it was first screened in the autumn of 2010. But it's glorious Highclere Castle in Hampshire which doubles up as Downton Abbey itself which is the real star of the show.

With its stunning acres of spectacular parkland, vaulted ceilings, panelled state rooms, 6,000-book library and priceless furnishings, family-run Highclere Castle is the ideal screen home of the aristocratic Crawley family around whose lives and those of their servants the Edwardian-set drama is based.

Above: A grand affair. The aristocratic Crawley family and their guests on the lawns of *Downton Abbey.*

Highclere which is home to the Earl and Countess of Carnarvon and has belonged to the Carnarvon family since 1679, doubles up as the interior and exterior of Downton Abbey, while part of the servants' quarters are a specially constructed set at London's Ealing Studios.

The kitchen yard of the house was partially built on the existing property but amazingly took just a few days to build. A little repainting was carried out at the castle using Edwardian colours and just one of the main bedrooms belonging to a minor character was painted a darker colour. Afterwards, everything was restored to its original state.

Highclere has been home to the 8th Earl and Countess of Carnarvon since 2001 and the home of their ancestors the Herbert family since the 17th Century, although records show the Castle stands on ground dating

Above: Magnificent Highclere Castle, home to the Carnarvon family since 1679.

back to medieval times. The Castle has been described by historians as "the perfect Victorian gem" and is well worth a visit if only to have a glimpse of some of the splendid rooms featured in the TV series.

Over the centuries the Carnarvons have lavished their wealth on remodelling 150-room Highclere, so making it one of the most spectacular family-owned mansions in the world. Structural changes to the interior of the Castle were completed in 1878 and it became a significant focus of political life during the closing stages of the Victorian age. Later, during the First World War, Highclere was used as a hospital for wounded soldiers and then doubled up as an evacuee base for children in World War II.

Aside from being the ideal filming location, it is used for corporate and private events including weddings. Celebrity couple Peter Andre and Katie Price tied the knot there in the opulent saloon which can be seen from the grand staircase and makes an appearance or two in *Downton Abbey*.

Like most privately owned stately homes, maintaining the 4000-acre estate has become increasingly costly and Lord Carnarvon has the unenviable task of finding the exorbitant sums required for Highclere's upkeep. Of course tours of the Castle along with hiring out its wonderful facilities help raise much-needed funds. Tourists may also be interested to learn of a remarkable Egyptian Exhibition which has transformed the castle's cellars, complete with a replica of the Tomb of Tutankhamun, a mummy, sarcophagus and a number of other treasures. It also includes an engaging 'tour' through the life of the so-called 'cursed' 5th Earl of Carnarvon who funded the search for the real Tomb of Tutankhamun. After many years it was finally discovered in the Valley of Kings by his partner Howard Carter in 1922. For details of visitor opening times at Highclere Castle and further information, go to www.highclerecastle.co.uk or telephone 01635 253210.

As fans of *Downton Abbey* will know, north Yorkshire towns including Ripon, Malton and Thirsk are referred to in the series, yet the village of Downton itself where the drama is set, is fictional and indeed could be anywhere.

"Finding the village was a huge challenge," said location manager Richard May. "Finding a village we could have control of to lose things like street markings and lamp posts and so on wasn't easy. We found a village called Bampton in Oxfordshire which proved perfect in the end. The villagers were fantastic, the nicest I've ever worked with actually. They were friendly and helpful and made everything possible."

Bampton proved to be the perfect location for Edwardian Downton. Before filming took place set dressers cleverly covered up street lamps with trees and bushes, yellow lines were disguised and the odd home was transformed into a shop or a pub, making the village look even more idyllic on screen. The local library was used for the entrance of the cottage hospital and pretty St Mary's Church appeared fairly frequently. Villagers enjoyed having the production team and some of Britain's leading actors in their midst and some were even fortunate enough to gain work as supporting artists, while others simply took the opportunity to watch the film crew from Carnival Films at work on their doorstep.

Other locations used in the drama so far include private homes in Bampton for the Rectory and Dower House and St James Park in London to where housemaid Anna, played by Joanna Frogatt, travelled while trying to learn more about Bates' past. When Bates arrived in Downton by train, the scene was filmed at the Kent and East Sussex Railway (www.kesr.org.uk). Horsted Keynes Station of the Bluebell Railway has also been used as Downton Station.

Waddesdon Manor (www.waddesdon. org.uk), which has been used recently as the setting for the Ridley Scott film *The Counsellor*

Right: (top) Samantha Bond plays Lady Rosamund Painswick with Dame Maggie Smith as Violet, Dowager Countess., *(middle)* Master of Downton Abbey Robert Crawley (Hugh Bonneville), the Earl of Grantham, *(right)* From left to right, Jessica Brown Findlay (Lady Sybil Crawley), Michelle Dockery (Lady Mary Crawley) and Laura Carmichael (Lady Edith Crawley), daughters of the house in *Downton Abbey*.

starring Brad Pitt and Michael Fassbender and A Little Chaos with Alan Rickman and Kate Winslet, doubled as fictional Haxby Park in the second series. This was the house Sir Richard was going to buy as a home for him and Mary, although the interior used was actually Halton House in Halton, Buckinghamshire, the officers' mess at RAF Halton. Hall Place in Wycombe End, Buckinghamshire was used for the interior of Mrs Crawley's House.

When Bates was in jail in York the scenes were shot in Lincoln Castle and First World War One trench scenes were shot at Akenham in Suffolk. West Wycombe Park, which has also appeared in *Lewis*, *Marple*, *Foyle's War* and *Cranford*, a National Trust property in West Wycombe, Buckinghamshire has doubled at the interior of Downton and Sutton's Hospital in Charterhouse Square, London which has been used for *Silk*, *The Mystery of Edwin Drood* and *The Suspicions of Mr Whicher* doubled as Ripon. Byleet Manor in Byfleet, Surrey was used as Dowager Violet's house.

Highclere is not the only castle to feature in *Downton Abbey*. 18th Century Inveraray Castle on the shores of Loch Fyne in Argyll, Scotland doubled up as fictional Duneagle Castle, home to the Marquess and Marchioness of Flintshire, in the Christmas 2012 special. The Granthams travelled there to spend time with their cousins

Above: (top) The staff of Downton Abbey line up to meet their guests, *(above)* Dame Maggie Smith as the formidable Dowager Countess of Grantham.

and were treated not only to the grandeur of the Castle itself, but to the surrounding spectacular landscape and lochs of the West Highlands.

Inveraray is home to the Duke of Argyll and his family and is open to the public between March and October. There are also two holiday cottages belonging to the estate which are available for rent. Go to www.inveraray-castle.com for further information or telephone 01499 302203.

Spring 2013 saw the start of filming of the fourth series, which was screened in the autumn. In addition to Highclere, the production team returned to Bampton for several weeks to shoot a variety of scenes including a wedding and the funeral of Matthew Crawley at St Mary's Church.

A feature length 2013 Christmas special saw the Crawley family decamp to their London residence for Lady Rose's (Lily James) coming out. Grade 1 listed Lancaster House in St James played Buckingham Palace while National Trust-owned Basildon Park in Berkshire doubled up as Grantham House although the exteriors were shot in London at Bridgewater House, Westminster. The staff's long-awaited 'away day' was filmed at West Wittering beach in West Sussex.

Above: (top) Inveraray Castle, *(above)* Horsted Keynes Station of the Bluebell Railway as Downton Station.

Sat nav references:

Bampton (OX18 2NE)
Highclere Castle (RG20 9RN)
Inveraray Castle (PA32 8XE)
Kent and East Sussex Railway (TN30 6HE)

Sat nav references:

Northwick Park Hospital (HA1 3UJ)
Wings (HA3 0QA)

Fawlty Towers
Bourne End

Sadly the real house used on screen as the infamous Fawlty Towers (shown in 1975 and 1979) hotel was bulldozed in early 1993. Wooburn Grange at Bourne End in Buckinghamshire, was ravaged by fire in March 1991 just before it was due to be renovated and was hit by a second blaze just four months later. Fawlty Towers hotel was supposed to be in Torquay in Devon but BBC bosses chose the Buckinghamshire site because it was nearer to London. After filming ended Wooburn Grange became a nightclub called Basil's and was later used as an Indian restaurant. By the spring of 1993 it had been demolished completely and had been replaced by eight five-bedroom family homes.

But *Fawlty Towers* fans can however visit other places associated with the series like Mentmore Close in north London where Basil beat his car with the branch of a tree in *Gourmet Night*. Just round the corner in Dovedale Avenue is St John's United Reformed Church which Basil was seen driving past in the same episode and the location for Andre's restaurant was 294 Preston Road in Harrow, which is now a Chinese restaurant called Wings. The hospital used in *The Germans*, where Sybil had her in-growing toenail removed, is Northwick Park Hospital in Northwick Park.

Foyle's War
Hastings

Foyle's War made its debut on ITV in 2002 and was considered an overnight hit. In fact it was the highest rated drama of that year, pulling in an impressive 10 million viewers and went on to win a BAFTA in 2003.

Written and carefully researched by Anthony Horowitz, who also created the ever popular *Midsomer Murders*, the crime drama was initially set on the coast of England during World War II and was shot largely on location in Hastings, Kent. Series one began in 1940 while the final series six, was set at the end of the war in 1945. Detective Chief Superintendent Christopher Foyle, played by Michael Kitchen, investigated murders and other serious crime and touched on subjects such as internment and conscription dodging in the process.

When ITV decided to axe the drama in 2007, there was a public outcry, so much so that there were strong hints that perhaps we hadn't seen the last of Foyle after all. And sure enough, filming resumed in 2012, only this time, not in Hastings but in Ireland.

Above: (left) A prop post box is carried into place *(centre)* Foster Place, Dublin *(right)* Michael Kitchen and Honeysuckle Weeks filming in Hastings. *Opposite:* Sam Stewart (Honeysuckle Weeks) and Christopher Foyle (Michael Kitchen)

The attention to 1940s detail was one of the most impressive factors of *Foyle's War*. The production team went to great lengths to make every scene as authentic as possible and all evidence of modern day life such as television aerials, satellite dishes, modern streetlamps and burglar alarms had to be removed or disguised from areas used for filming. And of course road markings, street signs and modern cars had to be hidden too.

Christopher Foyle lived in Hastings and it was here that a large chunk of all six series was shot. For instance, Steep Street was the location for Foyle's house and a genuine home — the actual address used was in fact 31 Croft Road, a rather narrow street in the old town. The house was privately owned and let out to ITV for filming purposes.

The High Street, Post Office Passage and Church Street also regularly cropped up in every series and like Croft Road, are narrow and restrictive and were usually closed off to the public while filming, not that residents raised objections. St Clements Church which can be found just off the High Street made regular appearances in *Foyle's War* as Sam (Honeysuckle Weeks) had to drive past it every time she visited Foyle at home. It was also used for a scene in the episode *The White Feather* where the characters attended a service on a National Day of Prayer.

The pilot of *Foyle's War*, which was made in the summer of 2001, was shot in old town Hastings which proved to be an excellent choice of location. The beautiful beach with its close proximity to France and historic links to the war led Anthony Horowitz to make his lead character a Hastings resident and so a firm bond between Foyle and the town was forged.

Historic landmarks, the fishermen's net huts appeared in some episodes as did Hastings Pier which first opened in 1872. The Royal Victoria Hotel, St Leonards was the scene of a murder following a bombing raid. While filming took place, the A259 which runs outside the hotel, was temporarily closed – no small feat as it happens to be one of the busiest roads in the UK.

Other locations used to shoot *Foyle's War* included Squerryes Court in Westerham, Kent, a stunning 17th Century manor house surrounded by 20 acres of historic gardens. Telephone 01959 562345 or see www.squerryes.co.uk for information on opening times.

The market town of Midhurst, West Sussex was chosen to film an episode in series five and locals recall seeing the actors huddled under umbrellas in the March of 2006 as the rain poured down. Several locations in the town were employed, including Midhurst Bookshop in Knockhundred Row which became a hairdresser's in the drama. The house adjoining the bookshop, Burgage House, was used as the Southern Bank.

Foyle's return to the screen in 2013 saw him move to London. Set in 1946, World War II was over and Foyle had been recruited into the intelligence service to help fight the Cold War.

But while all three two-hour films of the return series certainly looked like they'd been shot in the capital, they were in fact filmed in another country's capital city - Ireland's Dublin. Apart from the problem of the 2012 Olympics being underway while shooting was due to take place, London is a particularly expensive place for production companies. Furthermore, the landscape of the city has changed a great deal since the 1940s with modern buildings such as the Shard now nestling amid historic architecture, making it yet more difficult and costly to recreate a period drama.

In Dublin, the production team found the ideal backdrop for the London of 1946. The varied and versatile streets of the city doubled up beautifully for the quaint streets of post-war London, with two-storey Georgian housing and wonderfully adaptable civic buildings, helping to create an authentic look. Eleventh Hour Films which make the drama, based itself in Dublin itself and the production team was able to shoot the entire series within a 10-mile radius of the centre.

Above: (top) **The Four Courts, Dublin Above,** *(above)* **Actors playing soldiers on Hastings beach.**

Above: Michael Kitchen and Honeysuckle Weeks filming in Hastings.

The exterior of The Custom House, a neoclassical 18th Century building, doubled up as the exterior of MI5 headquarters and featured in all three films. The interior of MI5 was created in one of the buildings on the sprawling Clancy Barracks site which is situated on the south bank of the river Liffey. (Much of BBC drama *Ripper Street* was also filmed here.) The crew occupied the building for five weeks, having built offices, corridors and staircases which mirror the real MI5.

Other well-known Dublin buildings to feature in the series include the inner courtyard of Four Courts, Ireland's largest court buildings which became the inner courtyard of MI5 headquarters, Foster Place which served as the American Embassy and a nuclear bomb test scene - supposedly in Mexico - was actually filmed on a beach near Dublin.

If while watching *Foyle's War* you thought you spotted the Palace of Westminster and St Pauls Cathedral, you wouldn't be mistaken. Both buildings which scream 'London' appeared in the films thanks to the clever use of computer generated imagery.

Filming began on a further three films in January 2014, this time in Liverpool, Chester and Manchester, for broadcast in 2015.

Sat nav references:

Burgage House (GU29 9DQ)
Midhurst Bookshop (GU29 9DQ)
The Royal Victoria Hotel (TN38 0BD)
St Clements Church (TN34 3EY)
Squerryes Court (TN16 1SJ)

The Good Life
Northwood

The classic '70s comedy *The Good Life* saw Tom and Barbara Good turn their middle class home in Surbiton into a self-sufficient empire of vegetables and animals. At the time, it caused thousands to copy their idea and countless lawns all over the country were dug up and replaced by rows of carrots and turnips. Tom and Barbara's lifestyle, however, was far from ideal for their upmarket next-door neighbours Margo and Gerry Leadbetter, played by Penelope Keith and Paul Eddington, who awoke each morning to the sound of pigs and hens. In the series Kewferry Road in Northwood, Middlesex doubled for the fictional road, The Avenue, Surbiton, Surrey, because it was easier for the crew and actors to travel from the BBC Television Centre to Northwood with their cameras and props than Surbiton.

Sat nav references:

Kewferry Road, Northwood (HA6 2PQ)

Howard's Way
Bursledon

The BBC's '80s sex and sailing soap *Howard's Way* brought tourists flocking to south Hampshire where the series was filmed. It was set around the fictional village of Tarrant, played in real life by pretty Bursledon near Southampton. The series focused on the Mermaid Boatyard owned by Tom Howard and Jack Rolfe and that was played by the Elephant Boatyard in Land's End Road. You can still enjoy a quiet drink or a meal at the main pub used in Howard's Way, The Jolly Sailor just along the road. Halfway down Kew Road is Bondfield House, a private house which played the Howard family home in the series and just off Kew Lane is Hungerford where Hunt's

Above: Howard's Way was usually filmed in Hampshire, but this picture of stars Tony Anholt, Jan Harvey, Ivor Danvers, Kate O'Mara and Stephen Yardley was taken on location in Malta.

Folly played the home of Jan's mother Kate Harvey. The other major location was St Leonard's Church in Church Lane, Hamble, which was used for the filming of Lynne Howard and Claude Dupont's wedding.

The BBC was very resourceful in its use of locations to save money, for example the Victoria Rampart Jetty at nearby Warsash doubled as New York harbour when Lynne Howard crossed the Atlantic single-handedly, the High Street at Hamble played Italy in one episode and Waddesdon Manor, a National Trust property near Aylesbury, Buckinghamshire played Charles Frere's French Chateau Auban. Exterior shots of Victoria Rampart offices were also used as Ken Master's chandlery and Jan Howard's boutique and scenes at Ken's powerboat centre were filmed at a real-life showroom on the A27 at Swanwick. The business park built by tycoon Charles Frere in the series was actually Arlington Securities' Solent Business Park, just off junction nine of the M27 and the marina that Frere builds was actually Hythe Marina, at Hythe, near Southampton.

Sat nav references:

Elephant Boatyard (SO31 8DN)
The Jolly Sailor (SO31 8DN)
St Leonard's Church (SO31 8DU)

It Ain't Half Hot Mum
Farnham

You could be mistaken for thinking that the BBC comedy *It Ain't Half Hot Mum*, which was set in wartime Burma, was actually filmed in a hot sticky climate. But that was just clever make-up. For the series, which ran between 1974 and 1981, featuring the exploits of an army concert party, was actually filmed at BBC studios with the furthest location used being woods at Farnham in Surrey. And as with *Dad's Army*, the MoD allowed the BBC to film on its land, this time a wood. Clever set-dressing turned Farnham into Burma. Writer Jimmy Perry recalled: "We used to put rubber palms and rubber jungle creepers in the ground." The late Ken MacDonald, best known as barman Mike Fisher in *Only Fools and Horses* was thrilled when he was given the part of banjo-playing Gunner Clark, particularly at the thought of filming in some exotic foreign location. "But we ended up in these woods in Farnham," he later recalled, "but it was a great show to get into and tremendous fun."

Jonathan Creek
Shipley

Jonathan Creek, David Renwick's cleverly crafted mystery series was first screened in 1997 and ran fairly regularly until 2004, followed by occasional specials, the latest broadcast at Easter 2013.

The duffle-coated Creek — played by Alan Davies — is by no means your average television detective, managing to solve seemingly impossible crimes with the help of his crime writer colleagues. As such, it's quite apt that he lives in an unusual home — a windmill — not an easy find for the production's location scouts.

After much searching, the team discovered Shipley Mill in West Sussex which once belonged to the writer Hilaire Belloc and is now owned by a Trust. Tucked away down a quiet lane and overlooking a meadow, it proved perfect.

Despite its looks, it's actually the youngest — and the largest — windmill in Sussex having been built in 1879 for a Mr Frend Marten by Horsham millwrights Grist and Steele and cost £2,500. In 1906 the mill, nearby Kings Land house and the surrounding land were bought by Hilaire Belloc. With the advent of freely available electricity and motor vehicles, windmills across Britain began to be used less often as they became uneconomic to run.

Shipley Mill however combated this for a while by having a steam engine fitted that enabled it to be used on days when there was no wind and the mill continued to be used until the end of its active life in 1926.

Finally big roller mills put windmills like Shipley out of business. Between the wars Hilaire Belloc tried to keep the windmill in good order but the shortage of materials during the Second World War meant that by the time of Belloc's death in 1953 it needed considerable work to halt its decline.

An appeal was launched to restore the mill as a memorial to Hilaire Belloc and a local committee was formed which gained the support of the West Sussex County Council and it was reopened in 1958. In 1986 major repairs were again needed and a charitable Trust was formed consisting of various council representatives, the Friends of Shipley Windmill, the Society for the Protection of Ancient Buildings, the Book Trust and Charles Eustace, Belloc's great grandson who has given the Trust a 20-year lease at a peppercorn rent.

In 1990, thanks to grants and donations, the mill was re-opened, with just a single pair of sails, but a year later further donations meant a second pair could be added, restoring the mill to its former glory. Shipley Windmill is no longer open to the public although it may be viewed externally from the adjacent public footpath. See www.shipleywindmill.org.uk for details.

Above: (top) Jonathan Creek star Alan Davies on location at Shipley Windmill, *(above)* Stunning Shipley Windmill, the location for Jonathan Creek.

Lady Chatterley
The Isle of Wight

The Isle of Wight doubled for the South of France for the controversial 1993 BBC production of *Lady Chatterley* which starred Joely Richardson in the title role and Sean Bean as her gardener Mellors. The Old Park Hotel at St Lawrence (01983 852583) was the location for the beach and woodland walk scenes and the clifftop theme park, Blackgang Chine and Lisle Combe, the house at the Rare Breeds and Waterfowl Park at St Lawrence, played Lady Chatterley's father's south of France home, Mandalay. Havenstreet Station, part of the Isle of Wight Steam Railway, which runs from Wootton to Smallbrook Junction featured in the final episode when Lady Chatterley returned home from France. The final scene where Mellors and Connie embraced at the stern of a ship as they set off for Canada, was filmed on the Southampton to Isle of Wight Red Funnel ferry Cowes Castle which is now no longer in service with the company. The ship doubled as a cross-channel cruise liner sailing from Southampton water. It was picked because it had a traditional wooden handrail and by cleverly filming from different angles Director Ken Russell was able to make the ferry look like a liner.

Sat nav references:

Blackgang Chine (PO38 2HN)
Havenstreet Station (PO33 4DS)
Lisle Combe (PO38 1UW)
Old Park Hotel (PO38 1XS)

Making Waves
Portsmouth

In 2004, ITV had high hopes for its Royal Navy drama Making Waves - and so they should have. After all the Ministry of Defence had loaned producers a huge prop - Type 23 frigate HMS Grafton to play fictional HMS Suffolk and the show was blessed with a solid cast including former *EastEnders* star Alex Ferns (right) as Suffolk's CO. But the series bombed and unusually was taken off air before all of its six episodes had been screened. The cast and crew had spent many months filming the multi-million pound show in Portsmouth at the Dockyard and at other locations all over the city including the popular Gunwharf Quays shopping and restaurant waterfront development. For details see www.gunwharf-quays.com

Men Behaving Badly
Worthing

The town of Worthing in West Sussex featured heavily in the second episode of the final trilogy of the hilarious BBC comedy *Men Behaving Badly*, broadcast over three nights during Christmas 1998. The story saw Gary, played by Martin Clunes, having to attend a security equipment conference in the town and his girlfriend Dorothy (Caroline Quentin), pal Tony (Neil Morrissey) and his girlfriend Deborah (Leslie Ash) decided to join him.

They stayed at the aptly named Groyne View Hotel in Worthing, which wasn't the most romantic venue for a seaside break, especially when all four of them were sharing one room with peeling wallpaper. And while Tony, Dorothy and Deborah entertained themselves during the day with crazy golf, Gary became preoccupied with an attractive female delegate at the conference. Tony and Deborah stepped in to save Gary and Dorothy's relationship and the crazy golf course came off worst.

In real life the building used as the Groyne View Hotel isn't a hotel at all and is actually flats at 3-10 Marine Parade. It was the perfect setting as the building used to be a three-star hotel. The pier was used, as was the beach just to the east of the pier where Tony and Gary got drunk in a mock-up car. Flash Point, at the end of the promenade, was also used for the crazy golf course where Gary and Tony had a fight.

Midsomer Murders
Chilterns

The fictional county of Midsomer may well be one of the most idyllic in England but appearances can be deceptive: it also happens to boast the highest murder rate per manicured acre anywhere with one unfortunate resident after another bumped off at an alarming rate.

But as luck would have it, in the long-running crime drama series *Midsomer Murders*, there's always been a dependable detective on hand to find the culprit, in the shape of Detective Chief Inspector Tom Barnaby, played by John Nettles since the show began in 1997.

Above: DS Benjamin Jones (Jason Hughes), DCI Tom Barnaby (John Nettles) and DCI John Barnaby (Neil Dudgeon) in a rare appearance together.

In March 2011 Tom left for pastures new and his equally reliable and tenacious younger cousin John Barnaby (actor Neil Dudgeon) took over as DCI at Causton CID and is now solving murders which continue to occur at an alarming rate. Actor Jason Hughes who played his trusty side-kick DS Jones announced he was leaving in 2013 at the end of series 15 and Gwilym Lee has since taken over as DS Charlie Nelson.

Of course — and perhaps thankfully — there's no such place as Causton (the capital of Midsomer) but instead on screen it's created from several beautiful village locations spread across the Chilterns. Wallingford in Oxfordshire is a key location used to double up as Causton and has popped up in many episodes. For example, the Corn Exchange theatre in Wallingford has played as the Causton Playhouse, while Barnaby has been seen many a time, walking around the Market Square or motoring across Wallingford Bridge.

The village of Turville, Buckinghamshire, cropped up in *Murder on St. Malley's Day*, *Who Killed Cock Robin* and *The Straw Woman*. It's doubly interesting as the popular comedy *The Vicar of Dibley* was also shot there. When watching repeats of both shows, look out for the beautiful St Mary the Virgin church in the centre of the village.

Also in Buckinghamshire, this time in Beaconsfield, Barnaby and his team were found investigating a gruesome murder in Bekonscot Model Village which doubled up as Little Worthy Model Village in the aptly titled episode *Small Mercies*. Viewers will recall how the victim was discovered tied down among the tiny properties, Gulliver-style.

Equally at home on the cover of a chocolate box and in the same county is Long Crendon which featured in *Garden of Death*, *Tainted Fruit*, *Death and Dreams*, *Things That Go Bump In The Night*, *Dead Letters*, *A Tale of Two Hamlets* and *Second Sight*. Tucked away is the High Street with an array of quaint pubs, shops and cottages.

Waddesdon Manor, which is situated between Aylesbury and Bicester in Buckinghamshire, is a French-style chateau built by the banker, Baron Ferdinand de Rothschild featured in *Death of a Stranger*. With its splendid gardens, it is perfect for weddings, corporate events or just to visit. Go to www.waddesdon.org.uk for further information.

Several picturesque pubs have featured in *Midsomer Murders*, including The Cock & Rabbit in Lee in Buckinghamshire where Barnaby enjoyed more than a pint or two; The Crown in Cuddington which cropped up in *Death in Disguise*, *Death of a Stranger*, *Death and Dreams* and *Bad Tidings*; The Plough in Great Haseley, Oxfordshire; the renowned George and Dragon in Quainton, Buckinghamshire and in the same county, The Bell in Chearsley, which doubled up as The Woodman in one episode.

Not surprisingly with so many murders, there have been a fair few funerals in the deathly drama and an array of different churches used to send off the departed as well as for weddings and village gatherings.

Churches featured so far include Beaconsfield Church, Buckinghamshire which has been used as two different churches in different episodes; the interiors of Bray Church in Berkshire for a bell ringing scene; the 14th Century Brightwell Baldwin Church in Oxfordshire spotted in a few different episodes; the church at Brill, Buckinghamshire which featured in Four Funerals and a Wedding and St Mary's Church in Haddenham, Buckinghamshire which again could be seen in *Judgement Day*, *A Talent for Life*, *Birds of Prey*, *Orchid Fatalis* and *Vixen's Run*. Bledlow Church in the same county, doubled up as Badgers Drift Church in *The Killings at Badgers Drift*.

The secluded and pretty village of Bledlow also appeared in other Midsomer episodes, *Dead Man's Eleven*, *Blue Herrings*, *Dark Autumn* and *The Maid in Splendour* and interestingly, also in at least one episode of *Agatha Christie's Marple*.

The church of St Peter & St Paul in Dinton, Buckinghamshire which dates back to the 15th Century was used for a wedding scene in *Who Killed Cock Robin*, while in nearby Westlington Green, a body was found in a well in *Dead Letters*. On a happy note, at least for Tom Barnaby who rarely has much good news in his line of work, St Mary's Parish Church in Denham, Buckinghamshire, was used to film his screen daughter Cully's (Laura Howard) wedding to Simon Dixon, played by Sam Hazeldine in the episode entitled somewhat chillingly, *Blood Wedding*.

And don't forget, it's worth visiting all these beautiful villages for their wealth of history, interesting shops and quaint houses — all reasons which brought *Midsomer Murders* to their doorsteps.

Other locations worth mentioning include lovely Loseley Park near Guildford, Surrey (www.loseleypark. co.uk) where a large chunk of episode *They Seek Him Here* was shot in early 2008. The historic estate doubled up as Magna Manor, a shooting location for a film of *The Scarlet Pimpernel*. The director was found guillotined and Barnaby called in to track down the murderer. Estate owner Michael More-Molyneux said the *Midsomer* team used Loseley to the full, filming in its driveways and passages and stable yard which doubled up as a French courtyard complete with guillotine and chickens in cages.

Loseley is open to visitors to enjoy its surroundings and for celebratory and corporate events. Telephone the Estate Office on 01483 304440 for details of opening times.

Above: (top) DS Benjamin Jones (Jason Hughes) DCI John Barnaby (Neil Dudgeon) and Dr George Bullard (Barry Jackson), *(above left)* John Nettles and Jason Hughes filming *The Great and The Good*, *(above right)* Barnaby investigates a gruesome scene at Little Worthy Village, played by Bekonscot Model Village in *Small Mercies*. *Opposite:* Jason Hughes filming on location.

Above: (top) **A prop sign for Midsomer Herne,** *(above)* **Jason Hughes as DS Benjamin Jones.**

John Nettles' final *Midsomer* episode, *Fit for Murder* was set in a beautiful health spa. Sadly, there's no point in trying to book a getaway as the 'spa' is in fact a privately owned former manor house, now converted into a classically-designed office block just a stone's throw from Pinewood Studios in Buckinghamshire. Neil Dudgeon's first episode as DCI John Barnaby, *Death in the Slow Lane*, which kicked off series 14, employed a girls' private school near Reading as an exclusive school in the plot. The school (the head prefers it not to be named) was taken over by the production during the school holidays and interestingly was also used in a previous *Midsomer* episode, *Murder on St. Malley's Day*.

Neil's second *Midsomer* film featured a location fans can easily visit, Mapledurham House, Mapledurham in Oxfordshire. The estate doubled up as the home of an eccentric couple (played by Phyllida Law and Edward Fox) in *Dark Secrets* and boasts a working watermill which is well worth a look. Go to www.mapledurham.co.uk for details of opening times.

Among other locations used are Dorney Court, Berkshire, which has been used in several episodes including *Dark Secrets*, Buckinghamshire Railway Centre (seen in *Things that Go Bump in the Night* and *Down Among the Dead*); the Watercress Line, a beautiful steam railway which runs through the heart of Hampshire was used in *Echoes of the Dead*, Holloway College, Egham, Surrey, the Henley Regatta, the Tiptree Jam Factory in Essex, Chalgrove Manor, Oxfordshire and Chenies Manor, Buckinghamshire (www. cheniesmanorhouse.co.uk).

It was back to Chenies Manor for *The Oblong Murders*, which was also filmed in Long Crendon in Buckinghamshire including at the Eight Bells pub. The village of Warborough – a regularly used Midsomer location - was used for *The Sleeper Under The Hill* with the village pub The Six Bells making an appearance. Some scenes for *The Night of the Stag* were filmed at the Henton Mission Room at Chiltern Open Air Museum (www.coam.org.uk), The Crown pub in Sydenham and The Lodden Brewery in Oxfordshire (www.loddenbrewery.com) which played a cider mill. Among the locations for *A Sacred Trust* was the village of Aston Rowant in Oxfordshire. In *A Rare Bird*, the Cottage Bookshop in Penn, Buckinghamshire played a bookshop and The Lion's pub in Bledow played The Feathers. The civil war battle sequences in *The Dark Rider* were filmed at Knebworth House (www.knebworthhouse.com), Aldbury in Hertfordshire featured in *Murder of Innocence* as did the fire station in Rickmansworth. Incidentally, the former Rickmansworth police station in Rectory Road which was used as Causton police station was bought by the supermarket chain Lidl in the spring of 2013. *Written in the Stars* was filmed at Taplow in Berkshire and Watlington in Oxfordshire. *Death and the Divas* was filmed at Littlewick Green in Berkshire and Adwell in Oxfordshire. Locations for *The Sicilian Defence* included Warborough and at St Katherine's Convent in Parmoor, Buckinghamshire and scenes for *Schooled in Murder* were filmed in Turville and Shiplake College, Oxfordshire.

The team returned to the village of Long Crendon, Buckinghamshire for the 2013 festive episode, *The Christmas Haunting*, the first of five episodes that made up series 16 and introducing DS Nelson to viewers for the first time. Long Crendon Manor which has popped up in a number of episodes including *Things that go Bump in the Night*, *The Axeman Cometh*, *Death & Dreams* and *Not in my Backyard* played a haunted country house where Barnaby and his new sidekick investigated a fatal stabbing.

Sat nav references:

The Bell (HP18 0DJ)
Bledlow Church (HP27 9PD)
Brightwell Baldwin Church (OX49 5NS)
Buckinghamshire Railway Station (HP22 4BY)
Chalgrove Manor (OX44 7SL0)
Chenies Manor (WD3 6ER)
The Church at Brill (HP18 9RT)
The Cock & Rabbit (HP16 9LZ)
The Crown (HP18 0BB)
Dorney Court (SL4 6QP)
George and Dragon (HP22 4AR)
Loseley Park (GU3 1HS)
Mapledurham House (RG4 7TR)
The Plough (OX44 7JP)
St Mary's Church (OX9 3AJ)
St Mary's Parish Church (WD3 1JB)
St Peter & St Paul Church (HP17 8UG)
Tiptree Jam Factory in Essex (CO5 0RF)
Waddesdon Manor (HP18 0JH)

Mr Selfridge
Chatham

This glossy ITV1 drama based on the novel *Shopping, Seduction and Mr Selfridge* by Lindy Woodhead, is the true story of Harry Selfridge (played by Jeremy Piven) who transformed the world of retail by opening the first department store in London in 1909 - Selfridges in Oxford Street. But disappointingly, the glamorous interiors of this famous store seen on screen in 2013 are not the real thing but instead created on a massive set in Neasden, north London, while the exteriors are shot largely at the Historic Dockyard in Chatham in Kent.

The iconic exterior of Selfridges is a set, built on Anchor Wharf against the river wall. The only parts of the site which appear in the show are some reflections of the dockyard's buildings in the shop windows which is why the location was chosen, along with a few scenes filmed around the historic site. The upper storeys of the building are then computer generated.

Above: **Jeremy Piven as Harry Selfridge in** *Mr Selfridge.*

Above: The cast of *Mr Selfridge* on the specially-built set

While the set at Chatham stands for several months between series, filming takes just a few days. In the interim, the shop windows are boarded up, the revolving doors and signage removed and the whole set surrounded by wire fencing.

While this makes it difficult for fans of the show to see very much, the location itself is well worth a visit. It is of course where *Call the Midwife* is filmed and a historically interesting tourist attraction in its own right. For further information go to www.thedockyard.co.uk

Of course London itself is also used for the series with the entrance to a private residence in Kensington being used as the exterior to the Selfridge family home. Elsewhere, tube sequences were shot at the now closed Aldwych Station, which has appeared in dozens of TV and film productions including *28 Weeks Later*, *Superman IV* and *V for Vendetta*.

Gothic Strawberry Hill House in Twickenham was used as Chelsea Arts Club, the Theatre Royal, Drury Lane was where Harry swooned over Ellen Love and Richmond Theatre was used for the play which caused Harry lots of embarrassment. The Selfridges site prior to building was NoHo Square in London W1 (but it has now been built on in real life) and the temporary offices used before Selfridge's was built was the Farmiloe Building in Smithfield.

The interior of Lady Mae's house was the Defence College in Belgrave Square, the shop where Selfridge met Agnes for the first time was Langleybury House in Kings Langley and Bleriot's plane and pheasant shoot scenes were filmed at Stockers Farm in Rickmansworth, which has also been used for the filming of scenes for many television series and films including *Midsomer Murders*, *Bridget Jones: The Edge of Reason* and *Withnail and I.*

This page: The *Mr Selfridge* set at Chatham Dockyard.

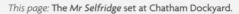

Sat nav references:

Chatham Historic Dockyard (ME4 4TE)

Mrs Brown
The Isle of Wight

Above: Osborne House, one of the main settings in *Mrs Brown*.

Much of the BBC's 1997 film *Mrs Brown*, which told the poignant and unusual love story between Queen Victoria, played by Dame Judi Dench, and her loyal Highland ghillie John Brown, played by Billy Connolly, took place at Queen Victoria and Prince Albert's real-life retreat, Osborne House on the Isle of Wight.

Victoria married Albert in 1840, three years after she had come to the throne and they bought the site in 1845 and replaced the existing house with Thomas Cubitt's design for a new home, the building that we see now. It was completed in 1851 and is now in the care of English Heritage. See www.english-heritage.org.uk for details.

The Royal couple found tranquillity at Osborne House with its fine views across the Solent and elegant Italian style away from the formality of court life at Buckingham Palace and Windsor Castle. Victoria said of it: "It is impossible to imagine a prettier spot."

Queen Victoria died on January 22nd 1901 on a couch bed in the Queen's Bedroom. The private royal suite was closed to all except members of the royal family until Queen Elizabeth II gave permission for full public access in 1954.

Of course much of *Mrs Brown* was filmed in Scotland. Privately owned 14th Century Duns Castle, on the Scottish borders near the market town of Duns, had a prominent role and if you fancy living like royalty, the castle offers accommodation and is available for weddings. See www.dunscastle.co.uk for more details.

Queen Victoria's waterfall picnic was filmed at a waterfall on the River Pattack near Loch Laggan. Other scenes were shot at Wilton House, Wilton, Wiltshire, which has also been used for the films *Sense and Sensibility*, *The Madness of King George* and *Pride and Prejudice*. See www.wiltonhouse.co.uk for details.

Osterley Park House, Isleworth, Middlesex, which also appeared in *Cranford*, was also used as was Luton Hoo, in Bedfordshire, a veteran of more than 20 films and TV shows including the Bond film *The World Is Not Enough*, *Four Weddings and a Funeral* and *Bleak House*.

Sat nav references:

Duns Castle (TD11 3NW)
Luton Hoo (LU1 3TQ)
Osborne House (PO32 6JX)
Osterley Park House (TW7 4RB)
Wilton House (SP2 0BJ)

The Office
Slough

Above: Crossbow House in Slough, used as the exterior for *The Office*.

When *The Office* made its debut in 2001, it certainly put Slough on the map with millions of television viewers — but perhaps not in a way that the Berkshire town's local council might have liked, as it doesn't exactly suggest it is a happening place. Of course Ricky Gervais and Stephen Merchant's brilliant workplace spoof fly-on-the-wall comedy was mainly filmed at Teddington Studios but the show's iconic opening title sequence was shot in Slough. The Brunel bus station and car park appeared (now demolished) as did the nearby Brunel Roundabout. The building on the Slough Trading Estate used for the exterior for the Wernham Hogg office in the opening titles was Crossbow House, Liverpool Road, Slough.

Sat nav references:

Crossbow House (SL1 4QZ)

Porridge
St Albans

Ball and chain jokes often feature at weddings at St Albans Register Office in Victoria Street, but that's perhaps predictable as it is housed in the former gatehouse to St Albans Prison. But the register office has an even greater claim to fame – it was the setting for the classic television comedy *Porridge* where Norman Stanley Fletcher did his lengthy stretch – between 1974 and 1977.

Above: The exterior for Slade Prison in St Albans - now a register office.

The real Victorian St Albans Prison, which had room for 85 men and 14 women, saw four executions, the last one being in 1914, but it hadn't been used as a real prison for decades when the BBC borrowed it as the front of HM Prison Slade. Designers put up the Slade signs, barred nearby windows and built a set of double doors at the end of the gatehouse entrance tunnel. The gatehouse was used after the Home Office refused to allow the BBC to film at an actual prison. Exterior scenes set within the walls of Slade Prison were filmed at various psychiatric hospitals around London.

It became St Albans Register Office in 2004 after being home to St Albans Highways Department for many years and offices have now been built behind the gatehouse.

The Home Office has relaxed its ban on filming in prisons since *Porridge* began in 1974 and now allows television companies to film in prisons for a fee, although much of the ITV drama hit *Bad Girls* was filmed at former Oxford Prison, which has now been converted into a hotel. See www.oxfordprison.co.uk for details.

Sat nav references:

St Albans Register Office (AL1 3TF)

Ruth Rendell Inspector Wexford Mysteries
Romsey

Most major towns in Hampshire were used at some point for the filming of the *Ruth Rendell Inspector Wexford Mysteries* which began in 1988 and ran until 2000. The country detective, played by veteran actor George Baker, was based at Kingsmarkham played by the town of Romsey near Southampton. The side entrance of the town's Magistrates Court doubled as the entrance to the police station with the production team adding just a sign and putting police cars in the car park to make it look like the real thing.

Many streets in the centre of Romsey featured in the stories and most restaurants and cafes were seen at some point along with the Job Centre, Romsey Abbey, the Corn Market and Palmerston Square. Two pubs, the Queen Vic and the King William IVth played Wexford's locals and the house that played his home was also in the town. Outside Romsey, St John's Church at Farleigh Chamberlayne was used for a funeral scene, an Indian restaurant called Kuti's in London Road, Southampton, was used for one episode, Sherfield Parish Hall doubled as a police control centre and Southampton University was used as Brighton University. Interior scenes for the story Speaker of Mandarin, which were supposed to be at a hotel in China, were actually shot at the Botley Park Hotel in Botley. The Kings Theatre in Southsea played a cinema and The Fuzz and Furkin pub, a former real police station, in Albert Road, Southsea, played a police station.

Sat nav references:

Botley Park Hotel (SO32 2UA)
The Kings Theatre (PO5 2SH)
King William IVth (SO51 8DF)
Kuti's (SO14 3DP)
Romsey Abbey (SO51 8EP)
Sherfield Parish Hall (RG27 0AA)
Southampton University (SO17 1BJ)

The Vicar of Dibley
Turville

Above: St Mary The Virgin Church in Turville, which plays St Barnabus in *The Vicar of Dibley*. *Left:* Two views of the beautiful village of Turville which plays Dibley.

The BBC comedy series *The Vicar of Dibley* became a huge hit for the BBC and its creator Richard Curtis when it was first shown in 1994. It starred Dawn French as Dibley vicar Reverend Geraldine Granger, whose pastoral work was at best challenging in a village full of quirky characters like Hugo (James Fleet), Alice (Emma Chambers), Owen (Roger Lloyd Pack) and Jim (Trevor Peacock).

Exterior scenes for the series were filmed in the Buckinghamshire village of Turville with the local church St Mary the Virgin, which dates back to the 12th Century, doubling as fictional St Barnabus Church. The exterior for the screen vicarage was actually two cottages in the village which were made to look like one house, but interior shots were filmed weeks later at the BBC studios in London, with a fake backdrop in place at the front door for continuity.

Turville is no stranger to film crews - it was used for the setting for the ITV drama *Goodnight Mister Tom* and appears regularly in *Midsomer Murders* amongst other shows. The nearby windmill, which overlooks the village, was used for the classic 1968 film *Chitty Chitty Bang Bang* and for the 1996 live action version of *101 Dalmatians*.

Sat nav references:

St Mary The Virgin Church (HP22 5SH)

London

The Apprentice

The Bridge Cafe in West Acton, London has seen a boost in trade since it's been used as the location where the losing team in *The Apprentice* are sent to deliberate. Frank and Jerry Marcangelo are thrilled that the publicity of the show has given their long-standing cafe more business. "I think they picked this one out because it's a working man's cafe and it's their punishment that they have to come here!" joked Frank. "It's definitely helped business - lots of tourists come here before they go up to London." The cafe, in Westfields Road, Acton, London, is open from 6.30am on weekdays so does a bustling trade in breakfast although *The Apprentice* candidates only get a drink while they are there, usually served by Frank. "I give them the drinks so I've been seen on TV a couple of times," added Frank.

Sat nav references:
Bridge Cafe (W3 0AP)

Ashes to Ashes

For the millions who adored *Life on Mars*, the follow up *Ashes to Ashes* was eagerly awaited and sparked an on-going debate as to whether the latter was as good as the former. Whatever one's opinion, this series paid just as much attention to period detail in its locations, being set in 1980s London as opposed to 1970s Manchester.

Above: Philip Glenister as DCI Gene Hunt, Keeley Hawes as DI Alex Drake and the famous Audi Quattro in a scene from *Ashes to Ashes*.

Life on Mars featured Sam Tyler, a modern detective who found himself back in 1973 after a car crash, and *Ashes to Ashes* worked on the same premise except this time, DI Alex Drake, a bright, feisty psychological profiler played by Keeley Hawes, was propelled from 2008 back to 1981. Here she teamed up with the ever-macho Detective Chief Inspector Gene Hunt (Philip Glenister) and theirs proved an often tempestuous pairing.

Three main locations which featured regularly throughout the series – CID, Alex's flat and Luigis restaurant - were all sets built at Kudos's production space in Bermondsey, south east London.

The exterior of the police station in *Ashes to Ashes* was actually shot at an empty building owned by the Stock Exchange on Christopher Street, London, by Finsbury Square. And conveniently, on the same street is a restaurant called Alexander's which played Luigis.

"With any exteriors you have to find buildings that are pre-1980s which can be anything from 100 years old up to 1981 so it can be quite difficult to find," explained location manager Mark Grimwade. "A lot of *Ashes to Ashes* was based around the river and the docks and to find those sorts of places which haven't been developed is pretty tricky.

"It was also meant to be based all around the Docklands area in east London and of course a lot of that has been developed. You just find certain streets which have parts that are still old fashioned and you have to be clever with the camera as to what you point at and what you don't."

Fans of the show will recall scenes on the River Thames which were shot near London's Royal Docks when Hunt and the boys raced to Alex's rescue on a speed boat at the end of the first episode. Old, disused mills doubled up as wharf-side buildings with Tower Bridge as the backdrop.

Other locations used include a club next door to Caesar's (London's oldest nightclub) in Streatham Hill. It was here that a gay club scene was shot. In another episode, the real Steve Strange, a club scene fixture in the 80s, was invited to the Blitz Club. This was in fact a snooker hall dressed to recreate the famous club and real Blitz Club fans appeared as very enthusiastic extras with '80's perms, shoulder pads or 'new romantic' costumes.

Sat nav references:

Alexander's (EC2A 2BS)
Caesar's (SW2 4RU)

The Bill
Merton

This popular police drama was axed in August 2010 after 26 years, during which time Sun Hill became television's best known police station. When *The Bill* began filming in 1984, the production base was a single-story office and warehouse complex in Artichoke Hill, Wapping in East London. In 1986 a redbrick Victorian building in Barlby

Above: **The exterior of Sun Hill police station in *The Bill*.**

Road, North Kensington became Sun Hill number two. When Thames TV's lease on the building ran out in 1989 the owners announced that they were going to turn the site into a shopping centre and *The Bill* had to look for a new home.

Production company Thames TV decided upon a former wine warehouse in Deer Park Road, Merton, which remained home to the long-running show until its demise. The new studio was bigger than the two previous ones and over the years extra sets were added such as a courtroom and the fictional St Hugh's Hospital. A street set was also added for Five's soap *Family Affairs*.

In 2010 the building became Wimbledon Studios and since then has played host to a range of productions including the Meryl Streep film *The Iron Lady* and the *Only Fools and Horses Sport Relief* sketch which featured David Beckham.

EastEnders
Borehamwood

EastEnders is a problem for location fans because there is very little for them to actually see as the show is shot almost entirely on a specially built set at BBC Elstree in Borehamwood, Hertfordshire.

The construction of the set took place between May and November 1984. The show's original design team wanted Albert Square where much of the drama is set, to look old and established and as authentic as possible. At the same time, they were concerned that the 'fake' buildings would not to be able to withstand the ravages

Above: It all looks so real - but Albert Square is a specially built set at a studio at Borehamwood, Hertfordshire.

of the British climate and didn't hold out much hope of them lasting more than three years. Little did they know, more than three decades later, the original Albert Square would still be standing.

Said the late designer Keith Harris: "After the hurricane of October 1987 I came to check the set with a feeling of impending doom. The roads were blocked with the fallen trees and when I got to Elstree the security guards told me the damage was pretty bad. Expecting the worst, I approached the set to discover that luckily it was virtually untouched by the violent storms - the security guards had been having me on."

The Albert Square houses actually have no backs as the interior shots are filmed at an adjacent studio. When the set was first built it had just three sides plus Bridge Street but over the years various buildings have been added including the bookies, Beale's Plaice, George Street and Walford East Tube Station.

EastEnders is a working set, so the BBC can't accommodate visitors, but fans can visit various locations used on the programme which aren't inside Elstree Studios. For example, Den Watts was shot by the side of the Grand Union Canal, near Water Road, London, Lofty and Michelle's marriage was filmed at the chapel in the grounds of Shenley Hospital, Shenley in Hertfordshire and Charlie Cotton's funeral, which coincided with the blessing of Ricky and Sam's marriage, was filmed at St Nicholas' Church, Elstree Hill. But most church scenes set in Walford are filmed at St Andrew's Church, Watford.

Pauline Fowler's and Frank Butcher's funerals were filmed at Hendon Crematorium in north London, Windsor Racecourse was used for scenes featuring Alfie and Kat, and Den's funeral took place at North Watford Cemetery, where a fake gravestone was put in place showing that Den was buried in the same grave as Angie. Walford's Register Office is usually Watford or Hendon Town Hall and if a court scene is required the location is in St Albans or Hatfield.

Above: Rita Simons (Roxy Mitchell) and Samantha Janus (Ronnie Mitchell) filming *EastEnders* on location in Weymouth, Dorset.

Over the years some episodes of *EastEnders* have been filmed abroad, in Amsterdam, Paris, Venice, Ireland, Normandy in France, Portugal and Marbella and Torremolinos in Spain and many scenes have been filmed in different parts of the UK including Blackpool, Manchester, Brighton, Portsmouth, Nottingham and Weymouth.

In January 2014 the BBC announced that it would be building a new set for *EastEnders* at Elstree. It said the new set would provide a modern, upgraded exterior filming resource for the show, replicating the appearance of the existing set but would be 20 per cent bigger to widen storyline possibilities and improve conditions for staff.

Sat nav references:

Elstree Studios (WD6 1JG)
Hendon (NW4 4BG)
Hendon Crematorium (NW7 1NB)
North Watford Cemetery (WD25 0AW)
St Andrew's Church (WD17 4PY)
Watford Town Hall (WD17 3EX)
Windsor Racecourse (SL4 5JJ)

Goodnight Sweetheart

The BBC comedy series *Goodnight Sweetheart* starred Nicholas Lyndhurst as Gary Sparrow, a man who juggled two women in different time zones, one modern day and the other during the Second World War. Unlike *Doctor Who*, we never saw how Gary managed to travel in time - he simply walked down a passageway off a London street and switched time. The passageway, Ducketts Passage, where he walked was actually Ezra Street near the flower market off Columbia Road, Bethnal Green.

Above : The Royal Oak which played the wartime pub in *Goodnight Sweetheart.*

His 1940's wife Phoebe, played originally by Dervla Kirwan and then Liz Carling, ran a pub The Royal Oak and its exterior was played by the real-life Royal Oak at 73 Columbia Road. The pub has also been featured in the film *Lock, Stock and Two Smoking Barrels*, the BBC series *The Hello Girls* and ex-*Eastenders* star Barbara Windsor popped in during her appearance in the BBC genealogy show *Who Do You Think You Are?* as her grandfather used to drink there. The modern day exterior of Gary's wartime memorabilia shop Blitz and Pieces was in nearby Old Street and the interior was a studio set. For more details go to: www.royaloaklondon.com

Sat nav references:

Royal Oak (E2 7RG)

Holby City
Borehamwood

Despite being a spin-off of long-running medical drama *Casualty* and supposedly set in the same fictional hospital, *Holby City* is filmed nowhere near Cardiff where Casualty is filmed. It is actually shot entirely on a purpose-built set at Elstree Studios in Borehamwood, Hertfordshire, also home to *EastEnders*. An office block used by BBC staff is used as one of the hospital's entrances. Occasionally, characters and storylines of the two series overlap and sometimes characters in one refer to a ward in another, but generally, the two series have separate identities.

Sat nav references:

Elstree Studios (WD6 1JG)

The Hour

The BBC drama *The Hour*, which starred Romola Garai, Dominic West and Ben Whishaw, took viewers behind the scenes of the launch of a topical news programme in London 1956. The drama, broadcast in 2011 and 2012, was written and created by BAFTA award-winning Abi Morgan, and mainly filmed at Hornsey Town Hall, an art deco former council building in Crouch End, North London. Hornsey Town Hall, which was used by Hornsey Borough Council as its headquarters until 1966, is Grade II listed which meant it was perfect for filming as most of its period features were intact.

Sat nav references:

Hornsey Town Hall (N8 9JJ)

London's Burning

Real life Dockhead Fire Station was used as the fictional Blackwall Station in the long-runnning ITV drama series *London's Burning* and played home to the Blue Watch crew. For the original 1986 90-minute *London's Burning* film, from which the series began, the whole of the Dockhead was used for filming. Makers London Weekend Television had full cooperation from the London Fire Brigade and the production team put portable cabins in the station yard for the real fire-fighters to use for the six-week duration of filming.

Above: Dockhead Fire Station the setting for *London's Burning*.

The cabins were used to replace the fire-fighters' relaxation area, the canteen, the mess and sleeping quarters while they were used for filming. In exchange for allowing their mess area to be used firefighters were given free meals on the catering bus. When a full series was commissioned, the production team built a full scale replica of the upper floor of Dockhead at Long Lane Studios in London. All exterior shots at Dockhead used the yard and the appliance bay. Because Dockhead was a busy working fire station (although it is currently due to be demolished and then rebuilt) the first priority of the film crew was to make sure they were never in the way when the real fire-fighters headed out on a 'shout'. For the last two series filming switched to Leyton Fire Station in Leyton, east London.

Love Soup

David Renwick's inventive comedy drama *Love Soup* shown in 2005 and 2008, starred Tamsin Greig as department store cosmetic counter manager Alice Chenery, whose struggle to find the perfect partner led her down a path of disastrous dates and embarrassing mishaps. If the department store used for filming looked real, it's because it was - it's actually House of Fraser's City branch, 68 King William Street. Because it is the City of London branch, it isn't open at weekends which meant that in addition to exterior shots, the interior scenes could also be filmed there. Before she moved to London, Alice lived in Brighton and the building used to house her flat was the attractive 1930s Furze Croft apartment block in Furze Hill.

Sat nav references:

House of Fraser (EC4N 7HR)

Minder

Even Arthur Daley was conned every time he went into the Winchester Club - because it was actually a studio set. But it wasn't always. In some early episodes of the popular ITV series, which ran from 1979 – 1994, about the exploits of dodgy dealing Arthur Daley, an actual drinking club in Chalk Farm, North London, situated next to the tube station was used. The outside door to the Winchester Club actually belonged to a building at 2b Newburgh Road, Acton, North London - but characters were never actually seen going through it because it led into a private flat. Arthur's car lot changed location over the years but the one last used by the Minder production team was at 89 Churchfield Road, Acton. Arthur's lock-up, where he kept all his dodgy gear, had changed since *Minder* began. For the last series it was at the rear of 7 Standard Road in North London. The pier that Arthur and Ray were always seen walking down during *Minder's* title sequence - was Southend Pier in Essex.

Sat nav references:

Newburgh Road (W3 6DQ)
Standard Road (NW10 6EX)

Peep Show

Channel Four's long-running comedy series uses the exterior of Zodiac House, London Road in West Croydon as the home to Mark (David Mitchell) and Jez (Robert Webb). For the first few series a real flat was used for interiors but for later series a purpose-built set was constructed in a studio.

Silk

Starring Maxine Peake, Rupert Penry-Jones and Neil Stuke, this BBC drama debuted in 2011 and followed a group of barristers, their cases and their individual ambitions, from the fictional Shoe Lane Chambers.

The series is penned by writer Peter Moffat who said he's based it on his own experiences at the Bar and as such, it's filmed almost entirely around actual chambers and court houses which adds to its authenticity. The main location which plays the exterior of the legal chambers is Goldsmith Chambers (right), a real barristers' chambers in Temple in the City of London. The interiors are shot within an old hunting lodge in Mill Hill.

As avid viewers will know, Martha's flat pops up several times in the drama but finding a suitable location didn't prove easy. The production snapped up what they thought was an ideal basement flat in which to film in Notting Hill but were eventually asked to leave after two visits.

"The residents of Notting Hill don't really like filming and a few people made life very difficult," location manager Rupert Bray revealed. "Although the flat we were shooting in had access to a communal garden, they didn't want us to use it. Even though I offered to make a charity donation to the garden committee, they flatly refused to allow us to put lights outside the window or cables in the garden. It just proved too difficult to service in the end so we then found another privately owned flat in St Andrews Square in Surbiton in Surrey."

As fans of Silk will recognise, the majority of scenes are shot in the Temple area, pretty much the same location in which popular legal drama Kavanagh QC was filmed in the '90s (and also used for *Pirates of the Caribbean: On Stranger Tides*). Nearby are the Royal Courts of Justice on the Strand where Martha, a criminal lawyer, appeals on a number of occasions.

Other courts used in the series are Kingston Crown Court which is currently in use and a real coup for the production team who were allowed in during the working week. They also used the old Crown Court in Kingston which is disused and the closed Magistrates Courts' at Dorking and at Shoreditch. "It's just a case of finding the right court," continued Rupert. "You can film at real courts at the weekend apart from the Old Bailey and certain criminal courts. The trouble is if you need more than one or two days you're stuck as they're then in session. So we were lucky as we managed to get in and out quickly and have access when we needed it."

Other locations to spot include all the pubs around Middle Temple which are normally closed at weekends, outfitters in the Temple (from where Martha's pupil stole a wig in series one) and the old Bird's Eye headquarters, Walton Court in Walton.

Sat nav references:
Goldsmith Chambers (EC4Y 7BL)
Kingston Crown Court (KT1 2BB)
Magistrates Court at Dorking (RH4 1SX)

Spooks

The first series of this long-running spy drama was screened by the BBC in 2002 and became an instant hit, going on to win a BAFTA. Set among a team of M15 intelligence officers (who are nicknamed 'spooks', hence the series' title) at Thames House in London, the storylines saw them battle all kinds of threats to the UK's national security from Al Qaeda to more homegrown threats. Peter Firth, Matthew MacFadyen, Keeley Hawes, David Oyelowo and Jenny Agutter starred in the initial six-part series followed in later episodes by a host of well-known faces including Rupert Penry-Jones, Nicola Walker, Richard Armitage, Hermione Norris, Gemma Jones and Sophia Myles.

Above: Jo Portman (Miranda Raison) and Adam Carter (Rupert Penry-Jones) go into action in a dramatic scene in *Spooks*.

Freemason's Hall in Great Queen Street, London which is home to the United Grand Lodge of England, doubled up as the exterior of Thames House, while the majority of internal shots in the 'Grid' where the team worked together on their latest missions, were filmed on a specially constructed set on an industrial estate in Bermondsey, south east London. Interior scenes had previously been filmed at a former university building in west London and then at Pinewood Studios. The design of the Grid was based exactly on the interior of the real Thames House.

Above: Freemason's Hall in Great Queen Street, London which played Thames House in *Spooks*.

Over the years, until its demise in 2011, *Spooks* was filmed across most of London but spilt over into surrounding counties such as Kent and Surrey where, for instance, an old Ministry of Defence complex near Chertsey doubled up as an American air force base. In another episode, a manor house in the same grounds was used as a secret hiding location for some of the characters.

Shooting in the heart of London with its huge, busy population of people and traffic is never easy, but location manager Thomas Elgood who worked on some episodes of the show said going the extra mile to obtain a certain look is exactly what made Spooks so eminently watchable. He admitted filming in London was a struggle but thanks to the popularity of the show, people were always willing to help when possible. Westminster Council, the police and the Royal Parks were particularly accommodating, he said.

Fans of the show may recall a major explosion at a central London hotel in one episode. This was in fact staged inside Wandsworth Town Hall, while the exteriors were of the Adelphi Building close to the Strand. Incidentally, there's a small street nearby which often stands in for 10 Downing Street in various television productions. Other central London locations used over the years include Forbes House in Halkin Street, Belgravia, which played the Iranian Embassy and with its grand exterior it was perfect as the Embassy's stately entrance. Several scenes were shot all around the Albert Memorial, the Royal Albert Hall and St James Park thanks to friendly assistance from the Royal Parks which welcomes television crews.

Further into the city at Moorgate, a sniper in one episode was seen taking aim from a tall building within City Point. And many scenes were filmed around the Old Naval College in Greenwich which with its tall Victorian buildings and pillars doubled up perfectly for the grandeur of the West End, particularly Whitehall. Clearly, in a long-running series such as *Spooks*, more and more locations were added every season and sometimes studios were required to film particular scenes. For instance, in series five, the final episode was shot at Action Underwater Studios in Basildon which required Adam Carter (played by Rupert Penry-Jones) and Ros Myers (Hermione Norris) to spend a great deal of time immersed in water.

2008 saw filming start on a *Spooks* spin-off series *Spooks: Code 9* on BBC3. Set in 2013, London had been evacuated after a nuclear attack and MI5 had moved in to set up field offices across the UK. Former Bradford police station The Tyrls was used for production and filming and many scenes were shot on location across Bradford and Leeds.

Sat nav references:

Action Underwater Studios (SS13 1DW)
Forbes House (SW1X 7DS)
Freemason's Hall (WC2B 5AZ)
Old Naval College (SE10 9LW)
Royal Albert Hall (SW7 2AP)
Wandsworth Town Hall (SW18 2PU)

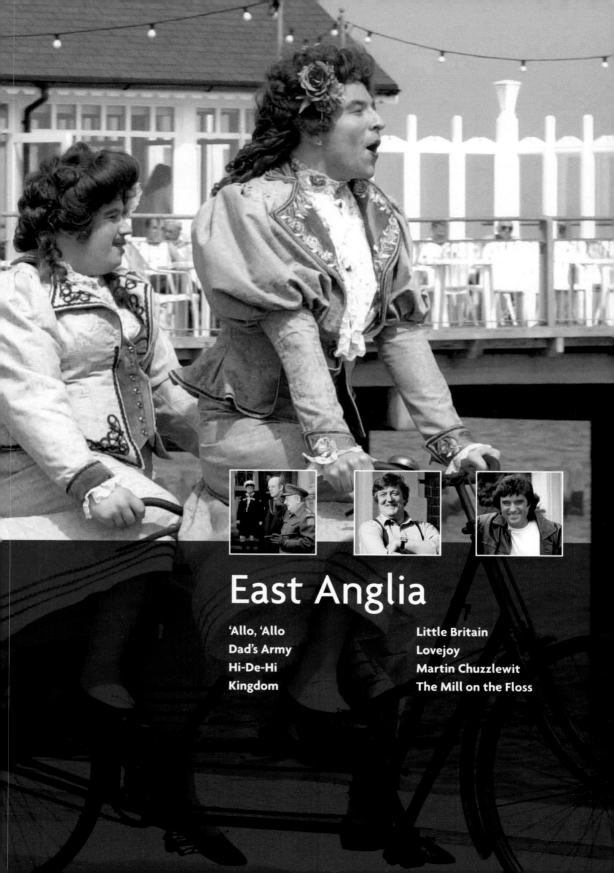

East Anglia

'Allo, 'Allo
Dad's Army
Hi-De-Hi
Kingdom

Little Britain
Lovejoy
Martin Chuzzlewit
The Mill on the Floss

'Allo, 'Allo
Lynford

The BBC found the ideal location to play wartime France in 'Allo, 'Allo, the popular comedy about the French resistance fighters, which ran from 1982 to 1992. For Lynford Hall, at Lynford in Norfolk was designed in the neo-Gothic style along the lines of a French chateau. So it was perfect for 'Allo, 'Allo and saved the BBC the expense of using a real French location. Lynford Hall was perfect for 'Allo, 'Allo because the front of the main part of the building was ideal to play Gestapo officer Herr Flick's headquarters and the cobbled courtyard round the back was easily turned into fictional Novienne square, including Café Rene. The BBC production team built the front of the Café and other Novienne shops over the front of the archways. Interiors were filmed in a studio. Lynford Hall is now a hotel and conference centre and has a licence for civil marriages. Further details are available at www.lynfordhallhotel.co.uk

Above: French-style country house Lynford Hall - home to Cafe Rene and Herr Flick in 'Allo, 'Allo.

Sat nav references:

Lynford Hall (IP26 5HW)

Dad's Army
Thetford

A German invasion force would have been completely foiled if it had tried to find Walmington-on-Sea, where Captain Mainwaring led his Home Guard Platoon in the BBC comedy Dad's Army. For Walmington-on-Sea was supposed to be a small town on the coast in Sussex. Yet the whole series was filmed between 1968 and 1977, in and around the Norfolk town of Thetford. Producers were lucky from the start because the MoD allowed them to use the Stanford Battle Area,

Above: They don't like it up 'em...the Walmington-on-Sea platoon charge.

a large nearby training area requisitioned by the army during the war. It was used for many scenes including the show's iconic closing credits. Bill Pertwee, who played Air Raid Warden Hodges, said: "We used it for a tremendous amount of locations, basically anything that involved chasing across fields like the episode with the barrage balloon, The Day The Balloon Went Up."

The cast and crew used to stay at the Bell Hotel and at the Anchor Hotel in Thetford. The streets of the town were used for filming and The Guildhall doubled as Walmington Town Hall in the episodes The Captain's Car and Time on my Hands. Much of the town was used including the Almshouses in Old Bury Road, which appeared in The Face on the Poster, Mill Lane where the platoon march in The Deadly Attachment and Nether Row, which appeared in four episodes: The Armoured Might of Lance Corporal Jones, Man Hunt, The Big Parade and Time on My Hands.

Thetford's Palace Cinema (now a bingo hall) featured in both The Big Parade and A Soldier's Farewell. Old Bury Road featured in The Face on the Poster and Mill Lane was used as the road to the harbour in the episode The Deadly Attachment. The pier at Great Yarmouth was used for the episode Menace From The Deep, and a disused airfield near Diss was also utilised. Sheringham railway station which is now on a preserved line and part of North Norfolk Railway, was used for an episode called The Royal Train. The Norfolk Broads were used for an episode Sons of the Sea.

Another memorable episode, The Two and a Half Feathers, which saw the whole cast playing out a long desert scene, was filmed at large sandpits at Kings Lynn. Drinkstone Mill at Drinkstone, Suffolk was used for the episode

Don't Forget the Diver and not far away is Wacton, setting for the episode *Round and Round Went The Big Wheel*.

Santon Downham was the site of the bridge used in *Brain Versus Brawn* and Brandon Station was the railway station used in *The Big Parade*. A National Trust castle, Oxburgh Hall, was used as Peabody Museum in *Museum Piece*. Kilverstone doubled up as Waterloo in *A Soldier's Farewell* where Captain Mainwaring dreamt he was Napoleon.

Lynford Hall was used as the backdrop to the shooting range in *Wake Up Walmington*, an episode which also featured the Six Bells, a pub in Bardwell, which reappeared in the episode *Ring Dem Bells*.

Above: Captain Mainwaring (Arthur Lowe) and the vicar (Frank Williams) outside the Guildhall.

Not strictly a television location, but one of interest to fans of *Dad's Army* is the pretty village of Chalfont St Giles in Buckinghamshire, which was used as the setting for the excellent 1971 *Dad's Army* feature film. Members of The *Dad's Army* Appreciation Society have staged tours of all these locations. For details, go to www.dadsarmy.co.uk See also: www.explorethetford.co.uk

Sat nav references:
Drinkstone Mill (IP30 9SP)
The Guildhall (IP24 2BA)
Oxburgh Hall (PE33 9PS)
Palace Cinema (IP24 2DT)
Sheringham Station (NR26 8RA)
The Six Bells (IP31 1AW)

Hi-De-Hi
Dovercourt

The BBC comedy *Hi-De-Hi*, set in a 1950s holiday camp, was another huge hit from the script-writing partnership of Jimmy Perry and David Croft. Broadcast from 1980 to 1988, the show starred the likes of Su Pollard, Ruth Madoc and Paul Shane. It was popular with the public but holiday giants Butlins were less than impressed and refused to let the BBC use one of their holiday camps for filming. Another company, Warners, had no such objections to the show and allowed the BBC to film at their holiday camp at Dovercourt, near Frinton-on-Sea. Sadly it was bulldozed several years ago to make way for a housing estate, although there is a section for touring caravans at the nearby Dovercourt Caravan Park.

Kingdom
Swaffham

The real life market town of Swaffham in Norfolk doubled as Market Shipborough in ITV1's popular comedy drama *Kingdom* which ran for three series from 2007 to 2009.

Stephen Fry starred as a country solicitor, Peter Kingdom, who set more store by human concerns than the law. Hermione Norris played his batty, man-eating sister Beatrice alongside a strong supporting cast which included Celia Imrie, Phyllida Law and Tony Slattery.

Although Market Shipborough was supposedly a coastal town, Swaffham is miles from the sea but a soundtrack cleverly gave the

Right: Stephen Fry played Peter *Kingdom* and is seen here on location in Swaffham.

Above: (left) **Oakleigh House, Swaffham, which played Peter Kingdom's office,** *(centre)* **St Peter's and St Paul's Church which appeared in** *Kingdom, (right)* **the cast on location.**

impression otherwise. Scenes of the quayside and the harbour were filmed at Wells-next-the-Sea in north Norfolk while Holkham was used for beach shots.

Kingdom fans visiting Swaffham will have no trouble spotting landmarks featured heavily in the series, particularly the town centre. The market place is a familiar sight as is Oakleigh House which played Kingdom's office. The Market Shipborough sign actually covered up the real Swaffham town sign during filming, while the town's Greyhound Pub doubled as The Startled Duck in the show.

Both Swaffham Methodist Church and St Peter and St Paul Church featured as Market Shipborough's local church while Swaffham's Church Rooms became Market Shipborough's Church Rooms. Swaffham Library also popped up as the local library.

Even some of the local shops got in on the action with a Break Charity Shop transformed into Tiger Lily's Sex Shop in one episode! Doves of Swaffham became a ladies clothes shop in another.

Other locations used included Swaffham Museum; Happisburgh village beach and cliffs; Denver Sluice in Kings Lynn, Norfolk and RAF Marham in Norfolk, which became RAF Fakenheath for two days for a storyline in which Kingdom investigated an American soldier serving in the US Air Force. Cockley Cley Hall doubled up as Aunt Auriel's house; racecourse scenes were shot at the famous Newmarket Racecourse and Queens College, Cambridge University appeared as Peter Kingdom's old college.

Sat nav references:

Break Charity Shop (PE37 7AB)
Cockley Cley Hall (PE37 8AG)
Doves of Swaffham (PE37 7LA)
Greyhound Pub (PE37 7AQ)
Newmarket Racecourse (CB8 0TF)
Oakleigh House (PE37 7QH)
Queens College, Cambridge University (CB3 9ET)
Swaffham Library (PE37 7DF)
Swaffham Museum (PE37 7DQ

Little Britain
Southwold

Old Haven, Darkley Noone, Troby, Sneddy, Herby and, of course, Llanddewi Brefi — they're the places where the weird and wonderful characters in the television comedy series *Little Britain* like Emily and Florence, Vicky Pollard, Lou and Andy, Dennis Waterman and Jeremy Rent, Kenny Craig and Daffyd lived.

And before you think that the hit show's writers and stars David Walliams and Matt Lucas invented names that are too wacky to be believable, keep reading — for the following six names are real places in Britain: Bozomzeal (in Devon), Blubberhouses (Yorkshire), Clenchwarton (Norfolk), Dull (Perthshire), Pratt's Bottom (Greater London) and Ugley (Essex).

For series two of *Little Britain* Old Haven, home to those would-be ladies Emily and Florence, was actually picturesque Southwold in Suffolk. Producer Geoff Posner told the local paper *The East Anglian Daily Times*: "It's perfect for Emily and Florence, the failed transvestites, who have a somewhat Victorian air about them - like Southwold!"

For the third series Eastbourne, East Sussex played the town and holiday makers out for a stroll were faced with two men dressed as women enjoying a ride on a carousel and the sight of Matt Lucas dressed as a baby. This time Posner

Above: *(left)* Emily (David Walliams) and Florence (Matt Lucas) enjoying a carousel in Eastbourne, *(right)* David Walliams and Matt Lucas film scenes from *Little Britain*.

told *Eastbourne Today* newspaper: "The characters Emily and Florence live in a Victorian world and the architecture of Eastbourne fits their world completely."

Scenes supposed to be Troby, where Lou and Andy lived, were filmed in various locations. For the third series a scene where Andy hopped out of his wheelchair and joined in a rugby match when Lou wasn't watching was filmed at London Skolars New River Stadium in White Hart Lane, London. Another sketch, when Andy did a parachute jump, was filmed at RAF Hendon, north London. Scenes of Lou and Andy's home were filmed on the Cranbrook Estate in Bethnal Green, London and the scene where Andy bought a snake was shot at a real pet shop, Magri's Pets at 205 Roman Road, also in Bethnal Green. Bubbles Devere kept that fabulous shape by spending lots of time at Hill Grange Health Spa in Trump, scenes for which were filmed at Gaddesden Place in Hemel Hempstead, headquarters of computer software company Xara. Gaddesden Place is a veteran location and has been in many films and television series including *Sharpe*, *Jeeves and Wooster*, *Jonathan Creek*, *Lewis* and *Foyle's War*.

The very striking former Royal Masonic School building in Bushey, Hertfordshire was used as Kelsey Grammar School, where Mr Cleaves taught. It has also been used many times for films including *The Meaning of Life* and on television for *Inspector Morse*, *Hex* and *My Dad's The Prime Minister*. Daffyd's village of Llandewi Breffi is spelt differently from the real village of Llanddewi Brefi (which has only one 'f') in west Wales. There were reports of attempted theft of village signs during the show's run between 2003 and 2006, even though no scenes were actually filmed there.

Sat nav references:

Gaddesden Place (HP2 6EX)
Magri's Pets (E2 0QY)
New River Stadium (N22 5QW)

Lovejoy
Long Melford

You might not bump into that loveable rogue Lovejoy if you head to Long Melford in Suffolk but you will find scores of genuine antique shops full of the sort of stuff Lovejoy would have loved to get his hands on. Long Melford, so named because of its particularly long high street, which is three miles long, was one of around a dozen in Suffolk regularly used for filming *Lovejoy*, the highly successful BBC series which

Above: *(left)* Belchamp Hall, which played Lady Jane's home, *(right)* Ian McShane as *Lovejoy*.

starred Ian McShane as the eponymous antique dealer. The attractive 16th Century Bull Hotel was regularly featured in the series along with many of the village's antique shops including Neptune Antiques and Ringer's Yard.

Over at Belchamp Walter, opposite the beautiful 15th Century village church with medieval wall paintings is Belchamp Hall, an elegant Queen Anne redbrick house, which was used as Lady Jane's home, Felsham Hall, in the series. The Hall is also available for hire for conferences, weddings and parties and the converted stables can be rented for holidays and short breaks. For more details go to www.belchamphall.com The attractive 300-year-old thatched Half Moon pub at nearby Belchamp St Paul was a familiar sight in the Autumn 1993 series of *Lovejoy,* which ended the following December, when it became one of Lovejoy's locals. Elsewhere many other towns and villages in the area were regularly used in the series including Braintree, Hadleigh, Kersey, Lavenham, Felsham, Sudbury, Halstead, Bildeston and Bury St Edmunds.

Sat nav references:

Belchamp Hall (CO10 7AT)
Half Moon pub (CO10 7DP)

Martin Chuzzlewit
King's Lynn

Above: **Peckover House in Cambridgeshire played Montague Tigg's home.**

Written in 1843, *Martin Chuzzlewit* was Charles Dickens' sixth novel, and filming requirements called for a labyrinth of tiny streets, supposedly in early 19th Century London. The BBC found the perfect location for its 1994 adaptation in the attractive Norfolk town of King's Lynn. The story centred on an inheritance and the contrasting destinies of the wealthy brothers Chuzzlewit and featured an all-star cast including Sir John Mills, Paul Schofield, Keith Allen, Tom Wilkinson and Julia Sawalha.

King's Lynn was one of England's foremost ports as early as the 12th Century and even today late medieval merchants' houses stretch back to the river between cobbled lanes and the famous Custom House. Those tiny streets proved to be perfect for the production team and where there were modern road markings, mud was used to cover them up. King's Lynn Council's offices doubled as Mrs Todgers' boarding houses and the frontages of cottages at King's Straithe, which also played early New York in the film *Revolution*, were used extensively. St Margaret's House and the lane next door appeared, as did the back of King's Street. "King's Lynn offered us the labyrinth of tiny streets that Dickens mentions in the novel," said Production Designer Gavin Davies. "I could get seven important locations within 10 minutes of one another."

Elsewhere, The Fleece Inn, a 14th Century pub in the Worcestershire Village of Bretforton, appeared as The Blue Dragon and a National Trust property, Peckover House in Cambridgeshire, played Montague Tigg's home. See www.nationaltrust.org.uk for further details.

Honington Hall, a 17th Century house at Shipston-on-Stour, Warwickshire, also appeared. The house, which has also featured in *Our Mutual Friend* and *Keeping Up Appearances*, is open to the public at certain times. For further details telephone: 01608 661434.

The Mill on the Floss
Bintree

Above: Bintree Mill, the main setting for *The Mill on the Floss.*

The BBC's 1997 adaptation of *The Mill on the Floss*, George Eliot's classic tale of unrequited love which starred Emily Watson, James Frain and Bernard Hill, who went on to play Captain Smith in the blockbuster film *Titanic*, featured a number of stunning locations. To find the principal location, that of the Dorlcote Mill, Location Manager Jeremy Johns visited 50 water-mills all over the country from Devon to the Lake District and from Wales to East Anglia. The interiors of Dorlcote – the corn-loft, milling-floor and sack chute – were found in another mill 16 miles away in Burgh-next-Aylsham and the kitchen and parlour interiors were filmed in an old farmhouse in Salle. Nearby were the locations for Lawyer Wakem's house and Lucy Deane's house, while the flood and rowing scenes were shot on a lake near Bintree.

The Midlands

By The Sword Divided
Market Harborough

Location managers could hardly have found a better location than Rockingham Castle for the BBC's 1983-1985 series *By The Sword Divided*. Set in 1640 during the English Civil War, the series followed the lives of the Royalist Lacey family and documents their involvement in the conflict. It starred Julian Glover as Sir Martin Lacey, Sharon Maughan as his daughter Anne Lacey, and Timothy Bentinck, famous on radio as David Archer in *The Archers*, as his son Tom Lacey, and ran for two 10-part series.

Rockingham was perfect as Arnescote and has been in the Watson family since 1530. The first Lord Rockingham, Sir Lewis Watson, was a Royalist, but his wife Eleanor was a Parliamentarian. The property had real-life experiences of the Civil War when it was badly damaged.

More than three centuries after the Civil War, Rockingham, which is still owned by the Watson family, saw Cavalier and Roundhead battles again when the BBC arrived. Rockingham Castle, which is licenced for civil weddings, is open to the public throughout the summer on certain days of the week. See www.rockinghamcastle.com for details.

Right: Stunning Rockingham Castle, still owned by the same family for nearly 500 years.

Sat nav references:

Rockingham Castle (LE16 8TH)

Doctors
Birmingham

Set in the fictional Midlands village of Letherbridge, *Doctors* is a popular daytime soap which first aired on BBC1 in March 2000. As the title infers, *Doctors* follows a group of medics, their patients and their families. Like the now defunct ITV police drama *The Bill,* appearing on the show is seen as a rite of passage for many a budding actor.

Until 2004, *Doctors* was shot at the BBC's Pebble Mill studios in Edgbaston, with real homes in the area doubling up as the living quarters of the medical staff and patients. The on-screen surgery was known as Riverside which later worked alongside another group of doctors based at the nearby Best Practice. When Pebble Mill closed down in 2005 and BBC Birmingham which produces the show moved into smaller premises, the Riverside was destroyed in the storyline and replaced with The Mill Health Centre. This is located at the BBC Drama Village in Selly Oak, Birmingham, on the edge of Birmingham University's Selly Oak campus. Complete with other fixed locations such as The Campus Surgery (part of the fictional University of Letherbridge), The Icon Bar and Letherbridge Police Station, *Doctors* is based at Archibald House, one of two historic buildings within the Drama Village. As before the move, privately-owned properties in the local area often double up as characters' houses with some houses belonging to long-term characters featuring on a regular basis.

Sat nav references:

BBC Drama Village (B15 2TT)

Endeavour
Oxford

Considering the success of its predecessors *Inspector Morse* and spin-off *Lewis*, it's hardly surprising that the pilot of ITV1's *Endeavour*, the prequel to *Inspector Morse*, was a huge success when it was screened in 2012. So much so, that a four-part series was commissioned immediately and was screened to critical acclaim in April 2013 - and it seems set to become a regular fixture in ITV1's schedules.

Above: Shaun Evans as *Endeavour* Morse

Endeavour stars actor Shaun Evans who plays Morse's younger self, an Oxford University drop-out who joined the police force and so begins a long, illustrious career fighting crime in one of the country's most historic cities.

Beautiful Oxford with its gleaming spires is of course the backdrop to *Endeavour*, although, as with *Inspector Morse* and *Lewis*, only five days out of each 24-day block of filming actually takes place there. This is largely because accommodating a large cast and crew in Oxford hotels is expensive. Most shooting is in London and along the M4 corridor, although on screen, you would never guess this to be the case.

The most high profile locations which feature in *Endeavour* are some of the colleges, namely the lesser known Regent's Park and Keble Colleges, both of which proved very accommodating to the production team. "It was the first time Keble had ever been used and as it's the only redbrick college in Oxford, it was enormously helpful to us," explained location manager Mark Grimwade.

As *Endeavour* is set in 1965, the centuries-old architecture of Oxford means less of a headache than some locations in producing a period drama. But the art department does have to wave its magic wand and make a few clever alterations to successfully transport us back almost 40 years. Yellow lines and other modern-day road markings are disguised, cars are removed and replaced with '60's vehicles and the odd door front is changed. Relatively little by some standards.

Scenes at Morse's flat are actually filmed at two separate locations. The interiors are shot at Langleybury Mansion, a dilapidated stately home close to Watford in Hertfordshire. Complete with sweeping staircases,

wood-panelled rooms and crumbling attics, the impressive site has become a popular filming location. It also has a children's farm attached to the mansion. The exterior of the flat is part of the Oxford University Department for Continuing Education in Wellington Square, while Southgate Town Hall in Enfield, North London doubles up as the police station - and both interior and exterior scenes are filmed there.

For the episode *Girl*, the row of shops featured was in Glebe Avenue, Ickenham. The funeral scene was shot at St Mary The Virgin in Hambleden, the hospital was Salesian College in Battersea and the large college dining hall used was in St Edmunds Hall College, Oxford. Pub interior scenes for this episode and the rest of the series were shot at The Griffin in Brentford.

The library in *Fugue* was the Old Library in Trinity College, which was also used for the rooftop sequence, the church interior was St Mary Magdalen Church in Oxford and the exterior St Edmunds Hall College, the piano recital scene was filmed at Trinity College and the doctor's house in a crescent was in Park Town, Oxford.

For *Rocket*, a Tate & Lyle plant in Greenwich, South East London doubled up for the arms factory, although part of the headquarters of the The Clare Foundation charity in Saunderton, Buckinghamshire was used as the entrance. The art deco house used was the modernist National Trust property Homewood in Surrey, (www.nationaltrust.org.uk) and the cloistered college was St John's.

In the episode *Home* Keble college looked stunning covered in snow and the entrance to the nightclub was the exterior of Regent's Park College in Oxford, whilst the interior was The Rivoli Ballroom actually 70 miles away.

The only intact 1950s ballroom in London, it's previously been used for filming of the videos for Elton John's *I Guess That's Why They Call It The Blues* and Tina Turner's *Private Dancer* (www.therivoli.co.uk).

A man was found in the road in Linkside, London, the railway station was The Bluebell Railway in East Sussex (www.bluebell-railway.co.uk) the college dining hall was in Keble and the pub where Morse had dinner with his sister was the Royal Standard of England in Forty Green, Beaconsfield, apparently the oldest freehouse in England, (www.rsoe.co.uk).

Sat nav references:

Keeble College (OX1 3PG)
Langleybury Mansion (WD4 8RW)
Oxford University Department for Continuing Education (OX1 2JA)
Regent's Park College (OX1 2LB)
Southgate Town Hall (N13 4XD)
Trinity College (OX1 3BH)
The Trout Inn (OX2 8PN)
The White Horse (OX1 3BB)

Opposite: Roger Allam as Detective Inspector Fred Thursday and Shaun Evans as Endeavour Morse.
Above: Shaun Evans on location.

Inspector Morse
Oxford

There is very little of central Oxford that didn't, at some time, appear in *Inspector Morse*, the award-winning detective series which starred the late John Thaw as the thoughtful Oxford sleuth. Some landmarks were easily recognisable from the television, but others, notably the colleges, were more difficult because often several different real locations were used to make one fictional place.

The King's Arms, known as the KA, on the corner of Holywell Street and Parks Road was one of the easily identifiable places - and was used by Morse to down a few pints of his favourite Samuel Smith's best bitter in several episodes. Just along in Holywell Street is the Music Room, owned by Wadham College, which was used in the 1993 episode *Twilight of the Gods* when opera singer Gladys Probert, played by the late Sheila Gish, gave a master class.

In Broad Street is the bookshop, Blackwells, where Morse was seen in several episodes buying books, and next door is the White Horse pub, another location where Morse could often be found drinking. On the other side of Broad Street is the impressive Sheldonian Theatre, where Oxford University confers its degrees. In *Inspector Morse* it was used in the episode *Dead on Time* when Morse took his ex-fiancée Susan Fallon to a concert there.

To the side of the Sheldonian Theatre, next door to the Bodleian Library lies the square used for *Twilight of The Gods* where a shooting took place. In Radcliffe Square, not far from Broad Street, is the unusually shaped Radcliffe Camera and next door to it is Brasenose College which appeared as two fictional colleges Beaufort and Beaumont in various episodes.

Above: (top) Beautiful rooftop view of All Souls College, *(above)* John Thaw and Kevin Whately pictured outside the imposing Radcliffe Camera, Oxford.

Seen from the beautiful Christ Church meadow is Merton College which appeared in the episode *The Infernal Serpent*. Christ Church itself was used as the backdrop to several episodes, and is very noticeable because of its distinctive Tom Tower. The porter's lodge at Pembroke College was used for the episode *Deceived By Flight* when Sergeant Robbie Lewis (Kevin Whately) posed as a porter to catch a murderer and a smuggler.

Out of the city at Wolvercote is the delightful Trout pub on the bank of the River Isis. It is from the bridge next to the pub that Morse and Lewis watched a frogman recover the Anglo-Saxon belt buckle, the Wolvercote Tongue, in the episode of the same name. The Randolph Hotel in Beaumont Street also featured heavily in the episode and also appeared in other stories. In addition, it was regularly used by John Thaw when he stayed in Oxford for filming and appeared in the film *Shadowlands*. Oxford isn't the only place used to film Morse though and in the episode *Masonic Mysteries* none of the city was used. Although on screen it looked like Morse rarely left Oxford, usually only five days of filming out of 25 took place in the city, with the rest of the days shot in other locations doubling as Oxford.

Above: An aerial view of Magdalen College and Bridge.

A territorial army centre in Southall, London, was used as the police station for the first two series, although for those series the front we saw on screen was the front of the real Oxford police station. For the third, fourth and fifth series a TA centre in Harrow played the police station and a Ministry of Defence laboratory in Harefield in Hertfordshire did the same job in the sixth and seventh series, but was demolished in the spring of 1993.

The front of the police station was not shown that much on screen as Morse and Lewis mainly used the back entrance. Morse's home was actually miles from Oxford. It was a ground floor flat in a Victorian block in Castlebar Road, Ealing, London. When Morse's home caught fire in one episode a set of the flat was built in a studio and burned, although fake smoke came through a broken window at the actual flat too. It was filmed in Ealing because it was cheaper not to travel to Oxford as it didn't involve an expensive overnight stay for the actors and crew. Many of the streets in Ealing look very similar to houses on the Woodstock or Banbury roads out of Oxford.

Stately homes were also often prominent in *Morse* including Cornbury Park in Charlbury, Oxfordshire, which was used for the episode *Greeks Bearing Gifts*, Englefield House, near Reading, which had also been used for *Jeeves and Wooster* and the mini-series *A Woman of Substance*, appeared in *Twilight of The Gods* and 14th Century Shirburn Castle was used for the 1994 episode *Happy Families*.

Another of Morse's favourite pubs, which was supposed to be near Oxford, was actually filmed at The Crown at Bray in Berkshire. The pictures inside the premises were replaced and they remain there today. The 1998 episode *The Wench Is Dead*, which saw actor Matthew Finney join Morse as his new sidekick Adrian Kershaw instead of Lewis, was filmed at The Black Country Museum at Dudley and on canals in Northamptonshire and Wiltshire.

The graveyard scenes – supposedly in Ireland – were filmed at Abersoch in Wales and a few extra fibreglass gravestones were added to real ones there. Morse spent most of the episode in Radcliffe Infirmary in Oxford and the scenes of him leaving were actually filmed there. The Radcliffe appeared again in the final episode of *Inspector Morse, The Remorseful Day*, which was first broadcast on November 15th 2000, as did the Randolph Hotel for a scene where Morse had coffee with Dr Harrison. Morse and Lewis met for their last pint at the Victoria Arms in Mill Lane Old Marston and at the end of the episode Morse collapsed and died of a heart attack in the quadrangle of Exeter College in Turl Street.

Sat nav references:
The Black Country Museum (DY1 4SQ)
Blackwells (OX1 3BQ)
Brasenose College (OX1 4AJ)
Cornbury Park (OX7 3EH)
The Crown (SL6 2AH)
Englefield House (RG7 5EN)
Exeter College (OX1 3DP)
The King's Arms (OX1 3SP)
Pembroke College (CB2 1RF)
The Randolph Hotel (OX1 2LN)
Sheldonian Theatre (OX1 3AZ)
Trout pub (SN7 8RF)
Victoria Arms (OX3 0PZ)
Wadham College (OX1 3PN)
White Horse pub (OX1 3BB)

Keeping Up Appearances
Coventry

The Coventry suburb of Binley Woods was the fictional home of social-climbing Hyacinth Bucket (or Bouquet as she pronounced it) and her put-upon husband Richard, in the hit BBC comedy series *Keeping Up Appearances*. The owners of 117 Heather Road, which doubled up as the exterior of the Bucket residence, thought it was a joke when a location manager first asked if the BBC could use the house for filming as they did not know that their neighbours at Number 119 had already agreed to let the BBC use their home as the Bucket's neighbours Elizabeth and Emmet's house.

Before filming began the production team used to put a fake garden at the side of the garage, extra plants in the existing flower border and add extra net curtains so the occupants couldn't be seen during filming outside. Patricia Routledge, who played Hyacinth, used the house's dining room as her make-up room but the interior scenes were filmed later at BBC studios. A few miles away, on a council estate in the Stoke district of Coventry, is Michell Close where Number Three played the home of Hyacinth's brother Onslow and his wife Daisy. The house was chosen because there is a scrapyard at the end of the road which was used as Onslow's yard.

Sat nav references:

Heather Road (CV3 2DB)
Michell Close (CV3 1DG)

Lewis
Oxford

Above: **Laurence Fox as Detective Sergeant James Hathaway and Kevin Whately as Detective Inspector Robert Lewis,** the stars of *Lewis*.

The spin-off of the hugely popular *Inspector Morse* first hit our screens in 2006 with Kevin Whately reprising the role of Robert or 'Robbie' Lewis, now promoted to Chief Inspector. *Lewis* was an instant hit and ran for seven series. Not only did viewers appreciate the tales based on creator Colin Dexter's characters but it was always fun to spot landmarks as, of course, the drama was set against the backdrop of historic Oxford. The series ran until 2013 and was still attracting solid ratings.

Many Oxford colleges including Wadham in Parks Road, Trinity, Brasenose, Lincoln, Exeter and Hertford Colleges popped up in several episodes of *Lewis*, with often just the exteriors of these beautiful buildings used to double up for other venues. Corpus Christi College was used in episode one of series two and the crew were even allowed to film a scene on a roof that was under construction. For that same episode, filming also took place at New College and University College where the Shelley Memorial is based.

Nick Marshall who was location manager on some *Lewis* episodes said colleges were always very accommodating to the production team, although the education of the students was never compromised. Therefore, it was important to try and confine shooting to university holidays – if possible. "Fortunately, Trinity allowed us to film for three and a half days during term time which was a great help," he revealed.

The well-kept grounds of virtually every Oxford college were ideal backdrops for Lewis and Hathaway, who were often seen strolling in these while discussing their latest case. Of course the distinguished, wood-panelled interiors of some of the colleges were also used in certain episodes. For instance, in *Old School Ties*, screened in 2007, the inside of a character's college room was shot at Merton College in Merton Street, while the porter's

Above: **The beautiful Radcliffe Camera in Oxford.**

lodge of her college was filmed at Oriel College in Oriel Street. The Principal's house of Hertford College also doubled up as the home of another character in the episode *The Great and the Good* in series two.

Nick was particularly delighted to receive permission to film at Oxford's renowned Bodleian Library in Broad Street which is the main library of the University of Oxford and is open to the public. In fact the library's Divinity Room and Exhibition Room attract over 200,000 visitors a year. For further information on the library, go to www.bodley.ox.ac.uk

In the final ever episode *Intelligent Design*, screened in February 2013, a body was found in a college chapel roof which was shot partly at Brasenose College where the production team was given permission to put up scaffolding outside. But as most Oxford colleges don't have attics, they had to 'cheat' certain scenes and the attic at Chenies Manor, a beautiful 15th Century Tudor manor house in Hertfordshire (www.cheniesmanorhouse.co.uk) which popped up in more than one episode of *Lewis* in various guises, was used.

There is of course more to Oxford than simply its seats of academia with the town centre itself, restaurants, hotels and stunning Botanic Garden in Rose Lane also featuring in *Lewis*. The Garden was established in 1621 making it the oldest botanic garden in the UK and the third oldest in the world. With thousands of species of plants, a magnificent greenhouse and walled section, it is a popular tourist attraction and well worth a visit. See www.botanic-garden.ox.ac. uk for more details.

Fans of the show will recall seeing the Bridge of Sighs in more than one episode. This is to be found in New College Lane and its official name is Hertford Bridge. The reason it is commonly referred to as the Bridge of Sighs is because of its strong resemblance to the bridge of the same name in Venice. It was designed by Sir Thomas Jackson, finished in 1914 and links the old and new quadrangles of Hertford College.

If you're planning a visit to the city, why not stop for a drink at the Turf Tavern tucked away in Bath Place which with foundations linking back to the 14th Century, makes it the oldest pub in Oxford. Lewis and Hathaway could be seen enjoying a drink in one episode at least, although the pair did not have a regular social haunt. If you do pop in, look out for the sketch of Inspector Morse on the wall.

Another Oxford pub worth mentioning is one that featured only in the final series of *Lewis* and had never been used previously in either Lewis or *Inspector Morse,* which is fairly unusual – Isis Farmhouse. A traditional, rustic pub situated on The Towing Path by the river, it can only be accessed on foot but is well worth the visit for its homemade fare. Lewis was seen there with Laura in *The Ramblin' Boy* in January 2013.

The Ashmolean Museum of Art and Archaeology featured in Lewis on more than one occasion. Situated in Beaumont Street, it was founded in 1683 and is one of the oldest public museums in the world, offering a variety of exhibitions throughout the year and better still, there is no entry fee. Go to www.ashmolean.org for further information.

Of course not all of *Lewis* was filmed in Oxford. For instance, West Car Park at Slough Railway Station doubled up as Oxford Station in at least one scene and Lewis's own flat was filmed inside a property in Ealing, while Hathaway's flat was in Shepherd's Bush, West London. Both were supposedly situated in Oxford. In series six and seven, Lewis's flat was shot at a property in Twickenham, while Hathaway's moved to Kingston. Obviously they were not seen to move on screen and both homes were supposedly in Oxford.

The attic of Swakeley's House (sometimes referred to as Manor) is in Ickenham, and is a 17th Century Grade II listed mansion which doubled up as the roof of Christ Church college. And Teddington School doubled up as an Oxford science faculty. The actual police station was Weir House in Uxbridge in the final series. Previously a set in Elstree was used to double up as the police station but it was pulled down at the end of series six.

Fans may recall Hathaway attempted to enjoy a rare break from policing in *The Ramblin' Boy* when he went to help out at an orphanage in Kosovo. The orphanage was actually the old RAF base at Upper Heyford in Oxfordshire while the Croatian farmhouse he was later dispatched to was in nearby Rousham Hall.

Fittingly, the last scene of the final episode of *Lewis* when Lewis announced he was going to retire and Hathaway said he wanted to try something new, was filmed at the Victoria Arms pub in Old Marsten. Interestingly, this is the same pub featured in the final episode of *Inspector Morse* when Morse and Lewis enjoyed their final pint together before Morse had a heart attack and died.

Middlemarch
Stamford

Producers of the 1994 BBC serial *Middlemarch*, which starred Rufus Sewell as Will Ladislaw, Douglas Hodge as Tertius Lydgate and Juliet Aubrey as Dorothea Brooke, quite expected to have to film in many different towns in order to authentically re-create Victorian England. That was because virtually nowhere exists unaltered since the 1830s. But that was before they stumbled upon beautiful Stamford in Lincolnshire and realised it couldn't have been more perfect a backdrop.

Above: (left) Rufus Sewell as Will Ladislaw in *Middlemarch, (right)* Stamford, the main location for the 1994 BBC adaptation.

The town needed some ageing so period-style doors were placed over new ones and Georgian-type windows were hung over the top of modern ones. Locations used in the town included unspoiled St George's Square, Browne's Hospital and the area Barn Hill - which includes Number Three All Saints Place, which played Doctor Lydgate's home.

Outside the town centre Grimsthorpe Castle doubled as Qualingham. The castle, which was also used for scenes in *Moll Flanders* and The Buccaneers, is open to the public for much of the year. See www.grimsthorpe.co.uk for details. The opening episode carriage scenes were filmed in Burghley Park. The Park is open all year and 16th Century Elizabethan Burghley House is open for much of the year. See www.burghley.co.uk for details.

Rambling Mill Lane and Stamford Arts Centre, which doubled as the White Hart Hotel, also appeared. In fact the Arts Centre, which also contains Stamford Tourist Information Centre, looked so much like a hotel after the BBC film team decorated it that several visitors to the town during filming tried to book rooms! In 2004 the building, along with St George's Square and St Mary's Street, appeared in the film version of *Pride and Prejudice*, which starred Keira Knightley and Matthew Macfadyen. This time the town played the village of Meryton, home to the Bennet family.

Peak Practice
Crich

Peak Practice became one of ITV's most successful drama series of the '90s. It began in 1993 starring Kevin Whately as Dr Jack Kerruish, Amanda Burton as Dr Beth Glover and Simon Shepherd as Dr Will Preston as the GPs at The Beeches surgery in the fictional village of Cardale. Over the years characters changed but it continued to be successful and ran until 2002.

The pretty Derbyshire village of Crich played Cardale and fans of the show can easily find plenty of locations. Even before you reach Crich marketplace you'll spot on your left, down the hill next to the Black Swan pub Archway House that played Dr Beth Glover's home.

Next you'll see the Costcutter shop which doubled as the bank in the series and a few doors along from that is the local fish and chip shop which was renamed The Cardale Fish and Chip Restaurant in honour of the series. The series' cast and crew often visited the shop while filming and Kevin Whately used to be a regular.

To find the house that played Dr Kerruish's home take a left turn down Dimple Lane, go on for about a quarter of a mile until you see fields on your left, carry on further and you'll find private Melkridge House that played his home. Not far away in Bobbin Mill Hill, Fritchley is Chestnut Bank House, a large private house which played The Beeches surgery in the series.

The pub where Jack Kerruish got involved in a fight in an early episode of *Peak Practice* was actually The Manor Hotel, in nearby South Wingfield. Nearby Wingfield Manor, a ruined mansion now owned by English Heritage was used for Cardale's medieval pageant. For further details about the house, which was also used for Franco Zeffirelli's 1996 film *Jane Eyre* see www.englishheritage.org.uk

The church where Dr Erica Matthews jilted Dr Andrew Attwood during the 1998 series was St Peter's Church at Edensor inside Chatsworth Park. Dr David Shearer was hit and killed by a motorcycle at Elton and the funeral was filmed at St Giles Church at Hartington. Outside Crich, locations all round the Peak District and in the magnificent Peak District National Park were regularly used.

Above: Wingfield Manor. *Below:* Dr Jack Kerruish (Kevin Whately) saves a life in a typical *Peak Practice* scene.

Sat nav references:

Black Swan pub (DE4 5DD)
Cardale Fish and Chip Restaurant (DE4 5DD)
Chestnut Bank House (DE56 2HN)
Costcutter shop (DE4 5DD)
Melkridge House (DE56 2HP)

Upstairs, Downstairs
Leamington Spa

The original series of this popular costume drama was broadcast on ITV between 1971 and 1975 and much to the surprise of some executives, gradually became unmissable television. A portrayal of upstairs aristocrats, the Bellamy family, and their downstairs servants, most of the drama took place within the elegant walls of 165 Eaton Place, an address in the heart of fashionable London during the Edwardian era and beyond to 1930.

The house itself, a tall, impressive building with polished steps and gleaming front door, not to mention vast interior rooms and huge hallway, formed a significant part of the drama series and for a while, the address was instantly recognisable by millions of television fans who grew to love the surroundings as much as the characters. The exteriors were actually of 65 Eaton Place in London with the 1 painted in front, while the interiors were filmed at London Weekend Television's studios in Wembley then at The London Studios on the South Bank.

Fast forward to December 2010 and *Upstairs, Downstairs* returned to television, this time on BBC1. The cast was completely different apart from actress and original creator Jean Marsh who reprised her role as Rose Buck. The residents were now Lord Holland, his wife Lady Agnes and their servants but the house in Eaton Place remained the same, albeit with a facelift. While Rose was a housemaid in the original series, she returned to Eaton Square as housekeeper in the later adaptation. Once again, the hallway was a feature of the house and to diehard fans the doorway couldn't belong anywhere other than to 165 Eaton Place. Anyone tuning in to *Upstairs, Downstairs* would have been forgiven for believing the exterior scenes of the impressive property were shot in the heart of fashionable London as they originally were. Remarkably they were actually filmed miles away at 42 Clarendon Square in Leamington Spa.

The search for the perfect Eaton Place spread across London, Bath, Bristol, Cheltenham and initially, only London appeared to offer any possibilities, though filming there generally proves difficult. The production team were flicking through books when the director suddenly said he'd spotted a stucco-fronted house in Leamington. So Clarendon Square was found by chance. Number 42 is someone's home and is

Above: Claire Foy as Lady Persephone Towyn and Ellie Kendrick as Ivy Morris. *Below:* London's fashionable 165 Eaton Place is actually an address in Leamington Spa, in *Upstairs, Downstairs.*

split into eight flats inside. The owner was abroad at the time but after being tracked down, agreed to allow the outside of his house to be used for filming as well as his hallway and front door. A false doorway was erected beyond the actual front door and the hallway was painted; very straightforward alterations.

The stunning interiors of Eaton Place were created on specially constructed sets in South Wales and designed by

Above: **Ellie Kendrick as maid Ivy Morris.**
Below: (right) **Filming** *Upstairs, Downstairs* **in Leamington Spa.**

Eve Stewart, Oscar-nominated designer on the award-winning film *The King's Speech*. The downstairs kitchen areas were built at Upper Boat Studios, Cardiff, while the main sitting room, the bedroom and the garage were filmed at Dragon Studios in Bridgend. The actual layout of the house is the same as in the earlier episodes with the staircase on the right hand side of the hall, all superbly designed by Eve.

Other locations of interest include the Ballroom at Claridges Hotel in London where the opening scenes of *Upstairs, Downstairs* were filmed and Mount Stuart Square in Cardiff, used to shoot political riot scenes. Cardiff University's Glamorgan Building doubled up as the Foreign Office, The Guildhall in Swansea became a railway station while the pub was especially built within the Coal Exchange in Cardiff.

Despite all the effort and excitement of this beautiful period drama, it proved to be far less successful than the original. After a number of script and cast changes, a second series was screened in 2012 but viewers were unimpressed and the BBC decided not to commission a further series.

Sat nav references:

Claridges Hotel (W1K 4HR)
Coal Exchange (CF10 5EB)
Glamorgan Building (CF10 3WA)
Leamington Spa (CV32 5QZ)
The Guildhall (SA1 4PE)

Vanity Fair
Warwickshire

Set during the Napoleonic Wars, William Makepeace Thackeray's classic novel *Vanity Fair* follows the lives of Becky Sharp, the penniless, orphaned daughter of an artist and a French opera dancer and Amelia Sedley, the sheltered child of a rich city merchant. They make a pair of unlikely but firm friends who are very different in character. Becky is an irresistible schemer and will stop at nothing to get what she wants whereas Amelia is meek and mild.

The lavish 1998 BBC adaptation of *Vanity Fair* starred Natasha Little as Becky, Frances Grey as Amelia, Nathaniel Parker as red-blooded Rawdon Crawley and Tom Ward as dashing officer George Osborne.

The series took 21 weeks to film and was shot in locations as diverse as London, Paris, the Rhine Valley and the coast of West Wales. The Ballroom scene was filmed at Cheltenham Town Hall and the town's Pittville Pump Room was used as a foreign restaurant for another scene. Both are open to the public and part of the Pump Room is now a museum.

The beach and several rows of houses in Tenby, Wales doubled as Brighton and Ragley Hall, Warwickshire, played the home of Lord Steyne. Claydon House at Middle Claydon, Buckinghamshire played the interior of a hotel in Germany. It is owned by the National Trust and is open to the public as are Stowe Landscape Gardens at Buckingham, Buckinghamshire, a stunning survivor of Georgian times which doubled as Hyde Park. See www.nationaltrust.org.uk

Sat nav references:

Cheltenham Town Hall (GL50 1QA)
Claydon House (MK18 2EY)
Stowe Landscape Gardens (MK18 5DQ)

Top: The beautiful Pittville Pump Room in Cheltenham.
Middle and bottom: Two views of stunning Stowe Landscape Gardens, used as Hyde Park, London in *Vanity Fair*.

Wales

Casualty
Doctor Who
Classic Doctor Who
Edge of Darkness

Gavin and Stacey
Our Mutual Friend
The Prisoner
Sherlock

Casualty
Cardiff

When *Casualty* was launched in 1986, no one could have predicted it would become television's longest-running medical drama, pulling in millions of viewers and winning several awards including a BAFTA for the best continuing drama in 2007. Set in Holby City Hospital in the fictional city of Holby, the series was filmed in Bristol until 2011. Over the years many city landmarks could be seen. For instance, the Clifton Suspension Bridge and the floating harbour made quite a few appearances.

Until 2011 most of *Casualty* was shot at a specially-constructed set inside an industrial warehouse in the St Phillips area of Bristol as it was decided early on, after the BBC's production team visited almost every hospital in Bristol, that trying to film a television series within a real-life working hospital simply wouldn't work.

For 16 years *Casualty* exterior shots were filmed at the Brunel College of Arts and Technology (now the Ashley Down Centre), part of City of Bristol College.

In 2002, a new exterior set was built at St Phillips, close to the interior set, so that virtually all filming could be done in one location. In 2011 the BBC decided to shift filming to Cardiff where a purpose-built set was constructed at the Roath Lock Studios, an impressive 170,000 sq ft site, equivalent in size to three full-size football pitches. The first episode from Cardiff was screened in January 2012.

While the majority of filming of *Casualty* now takes place at Roath, some scenes are shot on location in the Cardiff

Sat nav references:

Roath Lock Studio (CF10 4GA)

area. For example, a major car crash at a bus stop was filmed in 2013 just off Lloyd George Avenue in Cardiff Bay and other places used recently include flats in Loudoun Square and Fitzalan High School.

Doctor Who
Cardiff

Since its return in 2005 *Doctor Who* has been a huge success for the BBC - and a fantastic boost for the city of Cardiff where the show is produced. The production team has been very inventive and locations all over the city and in the wider area have been used to play both places on earth and further afield...

The Ninth Doctor — Christopher Eccleston

Series One (2005)

For *Rose*, Howells department store in Cardiff played Henrik's department store and part of University Hospital of Wales was used as Henrik's basemen. Much of the *The End of The World* was at filmed at the Temple of Peace Hall, Cardiff. The scene in *The Unquiet Dead* where the Tardis lands is White Swan Court in Monmouth, which is also where Beaufort Arms Court, which was used as the outside of Sneed's undertakers can be found. The New Theatre, Cardiff was used as the theatre where Dickens performed, the Exchange Building, Swansea was used for a street scene.

In *Aliens of London* Cardiff Royal Infirmary played fictional Albion Hospital, Hensol Castle, while Vale of Glamorgan was used as the inside of Downing Street. Hensol Castle appeared again in the second part of *Aliens of London*, World War Three. The long awaited return of the dreaded Daleks came in *Dalek*, most of which was filmed at the Millennium Stadium and at the National Museum of Wales, both in Cardiff. All of the next story, *The Long Game* was filmed in a studio but it was back on location for the episode *Father's Day* which featured St Paul's Church, Grangetown, Cardiff. Railway station scenes for *The Empty Child* were filmed at Barry Island railway (www.valeofglamorganrailway.co.uk) which was also used in the second part of the story, *The Doctor Dances*.

In *Boom Town* the Tardis landed in Roald Dahl Plass, Glamorgan Building of Cardiff University played city hall and various restaurants in Cardiff Bay also featured, as did Cardiff Central railway station. In *Bad Wolf* a flat at Severn Square, Cardiff played the Big Brother house. Some scenes for the *The Parting of the Ways*, which was Christopher Eccleston's final story, were filmed at Loudoun Square, Butetown, Cardiff, which was used as the Tylers' estate.

The Tenth Doctor - David Tennant

It was back to Howells department store in Cardiff, once again playing Henrik's, for David Tennant's first story *The Christmas Invasion* and back to the Millennium Stadium, a part of which was used as Unit HQ. Clearwell Caves in Gloucestershire (www.clearwellcaves.com) were used for the interior of the Sycorax spaceship.

Series Two (2006)

Worm's Head at Rhossili Bay on the Gower Peninsula was a stunning key location in *New Earth*, Wales Millennium Centre, Cardiff Bay doubled as the alien hospital and Tredegar House in Newport was used for hospital basement scenes. The production headed out of Cardiff for the next episode *Tooth and Claw* but although it was set in Scotland, it was all filmed in Wales with Craig-Y-Nos Castle hotel in the Brecon Beacons (www.craigynoscastle.com) playing Sir Robert's House, privately-owned Penllyn Castle, Cowbridge used as the courtyard and the National Trust's Dyffryn Gardens were used for the monk fight scene. Two schools were used for *School Reunion*, Duffryn High School, Newport and Fitzalan High School, Cardiff, Belle Vue Park, Newport was where the Doctor said goodbye to Sarah Jane. It was back to Dyffryn Gardens (www.dyffryngardens.org.uk) which played the Palace of Versailles in *The Girl in the Fireplace* and then over to Warwickshire where Ragley Hall in Alcester www.ragleyhall.co.uk was used for Versailles ballroom scenes.

Above: The Doctor (David Tennant) and Donna (Catherine Tate) in a scene from *The Runaway Bride*.

In *Rise of the Cybermen* the Tardis landed at the Riverfront Arts Centre and scenes where the president arrived were shot at Cardiff Heliport. In *The Age of Steel* Magor Brewery in Bridgend was where humans were converted and Uskmouth Power Station was the cyberfactory. For the next story *The Idiot's Lantern*, a shop in Blenheim Road, Cardiff, played Magpie Electricals and Florentia Street played Florizel Street.

The planet surface in *The Impossible Planet* was Wenvoe Quarry, Cardiff and it was back to Clearwell Caves in Gloucestershire for filming of *The Satan Pit*. Cardiff was heavily featured in *Love & Monsters* where shooting took place in many locations including The Hayes and St. Peter's Sport and Social Club in Minster Road. *Fear Her* featured Page Drive, Cardiff, the Millennium Stadium and St Alban's Rugby Club. Stunning Southerndown beach, Ogmore Vale, Vale of Glamorgan was the alien world in *Army of Ghosts* and Brandon Estate, Kennington, London and Loudoun Square, Cardiff, were the housing estates. MOD St Athlan, Brackla Bunkers, Bridgend and One Canada Square, London were used as Torchwood and the battle took place in Compass Bridge Road, Cardiff. Some of those locations were also in *Doomsday*. St John the Baptist at Trinity Street, Cardiff was the church in *The Runaway Bride* and the Baverstock Hotel, Merthyr Tydfil and New Country House Hotel, Cardiff were the locations of the wedding reception.

Series Three (2007)

Smith & Jones featured University of Glamorgan as the hospital interior and Singleton Hospital, Swansea as the exterior. It was over to Coventry for *The Shakespeare Code* where Ford's Hospital, Greyfriar's Lane and Cheylesmore Manor House portrayed London streets as did Lord Leycester Hospital in nearby Warwick (www.lordleycester.com) and Shakespeare's Globe in London played its original self. The Temple of Peace, Cardiff played the New York senate building in *Gridlock* and a regularly used location, Ely Papermill, was used for warehouse scenes. Scenes for *Daleks* in Manhattan were shot at a range of locations including the Park and Dare Theatre, Treorchy and Bute Park, Cardiff which doubled as Central

Park. Some of those locations also appeared in *Evolution of the Daleks* as did Treberfydd House, Llangasty, Brecon (www.treberfydd.com).

Wells Cathedral, Wells played Southwark Cathedral in *The Lazarus Experiment*, the Welsh Assembly Senedd building in Cardiff was the Lazarus Institute and the National Museum of Wales and Cardiff University's Biomedical Science Building also appeared. In *42*, Trident Park, Cardiff Bay and St Regis Paper Company Mill, Caldicot, both appeared. *Human Nature* featured Treberfydd House, Llangasty, Brecon, Llandaf village and St Fagan's National Museum in Cardiff were also used. Some of those locations were also in *The Family of Blood* and the battlefield scenes were shot at Neal Soil Supplies in Cardiff.

A former NatWest Bank in Bute Street, Cardiff was the police station in *Blink* and Alexandra Gardens in Cardiff was the site of the statues. Roald Dahl Plass in Cardiff made another appearance in *Utopia*, Argoed Quarry, Llanharry was the surface of Malcassairo and Wenvoe Quarry, Wenvoe was the rocket silo site. Hensol Castle was Downing Street in *The Sound of Drums* and other locations included Maelfa Shopping Centre, Llanedeyrn, Cardiff, MOD St Athan, Whitmore Bay, Barry Island and Penarth Esplanade. Some of those locations also appeared in *Last of the Time Lords* plus Vaynor Quarry, Merthyr Tydfil, Whitmore Bay, Barry Island, Roald Dahl Plass and Alexandra Gardens, Cardiff. The

Titanic lounge in *Voyage of the Damned*, the 2007 Christmas Special was The Coal Exchange, Cardiff Bay, and Exchange Building, Cambrian Place, Swansea was the titanic teleport.

Series Four (2008)

Helmont House, Churchill Way, Cardiff played Adipose Industries in *Partners in Crime* and the Fat Cat Café, Cardiff was the café. *The Fires of Pompeii* was filmed mainly on the set for the HBO drama series Rome at Cinecittà Film Studios, Rome, while the Temple of Peace, Cardiff, Clearwell Caves, Gloucestershire and Morlais Quarry, Merthyr Tydfil (which played the slopes of Mount Vesuvius). Lafarge Cement, Barry was the Ood compound in *Planet of the Ood* and Trefil Quarry, Tredegar was the Ood Sphere. In *The Sontaran Stratagem* and in *The Poison Sky* Margam Country Park, Port Talbot was the academy while the car went into the water off Compass Bridge Road, Cardiff.

The *Doctor's Daughter* featured Newbridge Memo as the human base, Plantasia Botanic Gardens, Swansea as the Source and Barry Shooting Range was the bunker. *The Unicorn and the Wasp* used Cefn Llwyd lake in Caerphilly, St Senwyr's Church, Cowbridge, Hensol Castle (www.hensol.co.uk) as The Harrogate Hotel and Llansannor Court as Edison Manor. In *Silence in the Library* Brangwyn Hall, Swansea was the library entrance and Central Library, Swansea was the library. *The Forest of the Dead* featured a range of locations including Hansol Castle, Glamorgan, Crwys Medical Centre and St Mary of the Angels in Cardiff, Dyffryn Gardens and Brangwyn Hall, Swansea. Midnight was filmed at Celtic Manor Forum

Above: Kylie Minogue takes a break from filming *Voyage of the Damned* in Swansea.

Spa, Usk Valley, Newport. *Turn Left* featured a host of locations in Cardiff including Bay Chambers, West Bute Street, Lady Mary Allotments, Roath Park, Cardiff Royal Infirmary and The Conway Pub. Porthkerry Viaduct in Porthkerry also appeared as did Avesta Polarit Panteg Steelworks, Newport which was the UNIT warehouse.

The Tardis materialised on Earth in High Street, Penarth in *The Stolen Earth*. Rose appeared in Queens Road, Penarth and Paget Road, Penarth, was where a Dalek appeared and shot the Doctor. Brook Street, Cardiff was where the Daleks rounded up humans and South Wales Traffic Management Centre, in Cardiff played UNIT HQ in New York. Southerndown Beach, Ogmore Vale, Bridgend made another appearance in *Journey's End*, Arcot Street, Penarth, was where Sarah-Jane, Mickey and Jackie surrendered to Daleks and Castell Coch in Cardiff played UNIT Germany. *The Next Doctor*, the 2008 Christmas Special, was filmed at Fonmon Castle, near Barry, (www.fonmoncastle.com) St Woolos Cemetery, Newport, The Maltings Ltd, Cardiff, MOD Caerwent, Monmouthshire, Tredegar House, Newport (the Doctor's base, and Tardis courtyard) Hensol Castle, Glamorgan Millers Green, Gloucester (when the Doctor arrived in Victorian London), College

Green, Gloucester (the funeral procession), Berkeley Street, Gloucester and Shire Hall, Monmouth.

Locations for *Planet of the Dead* included Gorsedd Gardens Road, Cardiff, National Museum of Wales, the East Tunnel, Cardiff, Mir Steel, Newport and the Dubai desert, UAE. Pentyrch, Cardiff was the suface of Mars in *The Waters of Mars*, the National Botanic Garden of Wales, Carmarthenshire was the Hydroponics Centre and Next Generation Data in Newport was the base. The book signing in *The End of Time* took place in Blackwells Bookshop, Cardiff University House, St. Mary's Church, Newport was where Donna got married, Wookey Hole Caves in Somerset was the Council of the Ood's chamber and City Hall, Cardiff, played The White House.

The Eleventh Doctor - Matt Smith

Series Five (2010)

For Matt Smith's first story *The Eleventh Hour*, St Cadoc's hospital, Caerleon, was the hospital exterior, Abertillery Hospital, Abertillery, the interior, The Vicarage, Rhymney played Amy's home and Lladaff village also featured. For *The Beast Below*, West Cross Anti-Aircraft Operations Room in Swansea was Churchill's Office and also appeared in *Victory of The Daleks*. Other locations included the rooftop of Cardiff University's Glamorgan Building, Jacob's Antique Centre, West Canal Wharf, Cardiff and Brackla Bunkers, Bridgend.

Southerndown Beach in Bridgend made another appearance in *The Time of Angels*, as did Clearwell Caves in Gloucestershire. Brecon Cathedral, Brecon was the museum. They also appeared in *Flesh and Stone* and Puzzlewood, Coleford, Gloucestershire was the Forest. Much of *The Vampires of Venice* was filmed in Trogir and Pantana, Croatia although some of the story was filmed at Caerphilly Castle, Caerphilly and Castell Coch, Cardiff. *Amy's Choice* was mainly filmed in Skenfrith and Sarn in Monmouthshire were Upper Leadworth and Llantwit Major, Vale of Glamorgan. *The Hungry Earth* featured St. Gwynno's Church in Llanwonno, Bedwellty Pits, Tredegar and Tower Colliery, Hirwaun. Locations for *Cold Blood*, Llandaff Cathedral, Cardiff, the National Museum of Wales, Cardiff, Trogira and Vrsine, Croatia and Neath Abbey, Swansea were used for *Vincent and The Doctor*. included Bute Park, Cardiff, St. Gwynno's Church, Llanwonno Tower Colliery, Hirwaun, the Temple of Peace, Cardiff, Plantasia Botanic Gardens, Swansea, Llandaff Cathedral, Cardiff, National Museum of Wales, Cardiff (as the Musée d'Orsay) and Neath Abbey, Swansea. Trogir and Vrsine in Croatia also appeared. Locations for *The Lodger* included two Cardiff parks, Mill Gardens and Victoria Park and Lanelay Hall, Pontyclun.

The *Pandorica Opens* featured regulars, the Millennium Stadium and Brackla Bunkers, Bridgend plus Stonehenge, Wiltshire and Margam Country Park, Port Talbot. *The Big Bang* used Puzzlewood, Coleford, Gloucestershire, Brangwyn Hall, Swansea, Miskin Manor and Margam Country Park.

Series Six (2011)

A Christmas Carol, the 2010 Christmas Special was filmed at The Coal Exchange, Cardiff Bay, Mamhilad Park Industrial Estate, Pontypool and Mir

Above: (top) **Freema Agyeman as Martha Jones,** *(middle)* **The Doctor (Matt Smith) uses his sonic screwdriver,** *(bottom)* **Karen Gillan in one of her first episodes as Amy Pond.**

Steel, Newport. *The Impossible Astronaut* used Tredegar House, Newport and Le Monde restaurant and Millennium Stadium in Cardiff. Other location filming took place in Utah, USA. Locations for *Day of the Moon* included Troy House, Monmouthshire, MOD St Athan plus locations in Utah and Arizona. *The Curse of The Black Spot* was filmed aboard The Phoenix, Charlestown, Cornwall and *The Doctor's Wife* featured Cemex in Cardiff. Locations for *The Rebel Flesh* and *The Almost People,* included Cardiff Castle, Caerphilly Castle, Neath Abbey, Swansea, Atlantic College, St. Donat's and Chepstow Castle.

A *Good Man Goes To War* used Millennium Stadium in Cardiff, Uskmouth Power Station, Newport and Lafarge Cement. Cyfarthfa Castle was used for *Let's Kill Hitler* along with regular locations Cardiff's Temple of Peace, and Brangwyn Hall, Swansea. Dyrham Park, Bath (used for the film *Remains of the Day* and the BBC drama *Wives and Daughters*) was used for *Night Terrors*. *The Girl Who Waited* used locations Dyffryn Gardens and Uskmouth Power Station. *The God Complex* was filmed at the Seabank Hotel, Cardiff and in Bute. Howell's department store appeared again in *Closing Time* as did Hensol Castle. *The Wedding of River Song* used many regular locations including Hensol Castle, Dyffryn Gardens and Bute Park. The 2011 Christmas Special *The Doctor, the Widow and the Wardrobe* used a range of locations including Stradey Castle, Llanelli (www.stradeycastle.com), Beechenhurst in Gloucestershire and Bute.

Series Seven Part One (2012)

Bute appeared again in *Asylum of the Daleks*, some of which was also filmed in the Sierra Nevada National Park in Spain. *Dinosaurs on a Spaceship* featured often-used Southerndown Beach but then the team travelled to Almeria in Spain for *A Town Called Mercy*. Locations for *The Power of Three* included Caerphilly Castle and Neath Abbey and for *The Angels Take Manhattan* a range of places in New York were used including Times Square, Central Park and Fifth Avenue. The 2012 Christmas Special *The Snowmen* used a wide range of locations including Treberfydd House (www.treberfydd.com), Treowen Manor (www.treowen.co.uk) and Insole Court, Cardiff.

Series Seven Part Two (2013)

Locations for *The Bells of Saint John* included Southerndown Beach, Caerphilly Castle and The Grange St Pauls Hotel in London and for *The Rings of Akhaten*, St Woolos Cemetery in Newport. Most of *Cold War* was filmed in the studio

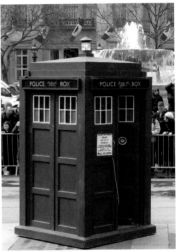

Above: (top) Jenna-Louise Coleman filming at Chepstow Castle, *(above)* The Tardis in Trafalgar Square for the 50th anniversary episode.

although a small amount was shot at Port Teigr. *Hide* used a range of locations including Margam Country Park, Gethin Woodland Park, the National Trust house Tyntesfield and The Manor of Plas Llanmihangel. Most of *Journey to the Centre of the TARDIS* was filmed at the BBC's Roath Lock studios but one scene was filmed at Argoed Isha Quarry, Llansannor. A range of locations were used for *The Crimson Horror* including the town of Llantrisant and Holy Trinity Presbyterian Church in Barry. Regular locations Castle Coch, Caerphilly Castle, The Coal Exchange and City Hall, Cardiff all featured in *Nightmare in Silver* and other regulars appeared in *The Name of the Doctor* including Cardiff Castle, Neath Abbey, Swansea plus Merthyr Mawr Warren reserve near Bridgend. The 50th Anniversary Special locations included Trafalgar Square and The Tower of London, Ivy Tower, Neath and Chepstow Castle.

Classic Doctor Who

In the 50 years since Doctor Who began, the time travelling Doctor has been all over the galaxy - without leaving Earth! Credit must go to the show's many location managers who, over the years, have managed to find dozens of British locations to play either far-off planets or Earth in the past, present or future. What follows are some of the more interesting locations used over the years for filming of the classic series of Doctor Who - but clearly it is not an exhaustive list.

Above: Jon Pertwee on location in Portsmouth for the filming of *The Sea Devils.*

The First Doctor - William Hartnell *(1963-1966)*

Back in 1964, when the late William Hartnell played the Doctor, the dreaded Daleks invaded the planet in the story *The Dalek Invasion of Earth* and were seen roaming in London near the Houses of Parliament, in Trafalgar Square, on Westminster Bridge, on the South Bank, at Whitehall and at the Albert Memorial. The footage shot in Trafalgar Square was shot at 5am and was supposed to show a deserted London where everyone was hiding away from the Daleks. It looked deserted - except that if you looked very carefully you could see a bus! The 1966 story *The Smugglers* was filmed at Nanjizal Bay in Cornwall.

The Second Doctor - Patrick Troughton *(1966-1969)*

Doctor number two, played by the late Patrick Troughton, landed his Tardis at Gatwick Airport in the story *The Faceless Ones*. The Nant Ffrancon Pass and Ogwen Lake in Snowdonia, Wales, played a more exotic location: Tibet, home of the Yeti - or so it appeared - in the 1967 story *The Abominable Snowman*. But when the Yeti took over the London underground in *The Web of Fear*, London Transport demanded so high a fee for the use of its tube tunnels - and then only in the early hours of the morning - that the BBC filmed most of the story on studio sets. Climping Beach, Littlehampton, West Sussex was used for *The Enemy of the World*. The series took to the sea - well, the Thames Estuary - for the 1968 story *Fury From The Deep*, filming on the Radio 390 Offshore Platform at Red Sands and on the beach at Kingsgate in Kent. One of the series' most visually spectacular location sequences came in the 1968 story *The Invasion* when a supposedly massive army of Cybermen swept into London. After emerging from sewers, the Cybermen were later seen descending the steps with St Paul's Cathedral in the background. The quarries seen in *The Krotons* were in Malvern, Worcestershire and a string of locations in West Sussex including Clayton and East and West Dean were used for *The War Games*.

The Third Doctor - Jon Pertwee *(1970-1974)*

When the late Jon Pertwee took over the role of the Doctor in 1970 he came face to face in his first adventure with plastic monsters, the Autons, in *Spearhead from Space*. In another eerie sequence, the Autons, in the guise of tailors' dummies, came alive in a shop window, smashed their way out and started walking down the street shooting people. This scene was filmed early one Sunday morning in Ealing High Street in north London. The inside of Madame Tussauds in London was also used for a scene. The story also called for scenes at a hospital and at the headquarters of the United Nations Intelligence Task Force (UNIT) - and these were shot at the BBC's Engineering Training Centre at Wood Norton, near Evesham. In the 1971 story *The Mind of Evil*, Dover Castle played a prison where the evil Master, played by Roger Delgado, was being kept under lock and key. During the story prisoners took over the prison and the authorities sent in UNIT troops to storm it in one of the programme's finest action sequences. Later that year the Wiltshire village of Aldbourne played the fictional village of Devil's End in the popular story *The Daemons*. The village pub, The Blue Boar, doubled as The Cloven Hoof and the village church was used as the church. The barrow, which played Devil's Hump in the series, is about 1/4 of a mile from Aldbourne up a dirt track. Aldbourne was where Easy Company, part of the US 101st Airborne Division, depicted in *Band of Brothers*, were based during World War Two. The 1972 story *The Sea Devils* used 19th Century No Man's Land Fort in the sea between Portsmouth and the Isle of Wight. The Royal Navy helped the BBC with *The Sea Devils* and allowed them to use its Whale Island base, HMS Excellent, in Portsmouth as the fictional HMS Seaspite, and also Frazer Gunnery Range. Norris Castle on the Isle of Wight was used as a prison for the dastardly villain, The Master. In the 1973 story *The Three Doctors*, Denham Manor, Denham, Buckinghamshire became UNIT headquarters and some footage of William Hartnell, who was too ill to film in London, was recorded in the garden of his home in Mayfield, Sussex. *The Time Warrior* was filmed at Peckforton Castle in Cheshire (see www.peckfortoncastle.co.uk) and *The Green Death* was filmed at a colliery, now Darran Valley country park in Deri, Glamorgan.

Above: Sarah-Jane Smith (Elisabeth Sladen) tries to escape from Linx, a sontaran in *The Time Warrior*

The Fourth Doctor - Tom Baker *(1975-1981)*

Tom Baker's first story *Robot* was filmed at Wood Norton Hall in Worcestershire and other locations in his first season include: Hound Tor on Dartmoor (*The Sontaran Experiment*) and Wookey Hole caves at Wells in Somerset (*Revenge of the Cybermen*). Scotland was the setting for *The Terror Of The Zygons* but the BBC decided to film much of it in West Sussex. Among the key locations was a pub, The Fox Goes Free at Charlton. Athelhampton House, near Dorchester in Dorset, was the location for the 1976 adventure *The Seeds of Doom* and had also been used for *Sleuth* which starred Michael Caine and Laurence Olivier. Mick Jagger's former home, Stargroves, at East End near Newbury, was used in stories *The Pyramids Of Mars* and *The Image of The Fendahl*. Tom Baker's final scenes in *Logopolis* were filmed at the BBC receiving station in Crowsley Park, Berkshire which played the Pharos Project.

The Fifth Doctor - Peter Davison *(1982-1984)*

Peter Davison, the fifth Doctor, filmed some of his first story *Castrovalva* at Harrison's Rock, Groombridge, East Sussex, *The Visitation* was filmed at Black Park, near Fulmer in Buckinghamshire (also used for the Tom Baker story *Full Circle*, the Sylvester McCoy story *Battlefield* as well as several *Harry Potter* films, the Bond film *Casino Royale* and *Batman*) and some of *Time-Flight* at Heathrow Airport. *Mawdryn Undead* was filmed at Middlesex University, Trent Park, Barnet, *The King's Demons* at Bodiam Castle, East Sussex and *The Awakening* at Shapwick in Dorset. Much of the 1984 story *The Resurrection of The Daleks* was filmed in Shad Thames in the London Docklands. Much of the 1983 20th Anniversary show, *The Five Doctors*, was filmed in North Wales (including at a quarry at Blaenau Ffestiniog), although one of Jon Pertwee's sequences in his car, Bessie, was filmed in Denham. Footage of Tom Baker, who didn't take part in the episode, was taken from the 1979 story *Shada*, which had never been finished because of a BBC strike. In the sequences, the Doctor and his assistant Romana, played by Lalla Ward, were seen punting on the river in Cambridge.

The Sixth Doctor - Colin Baker *(1984-1986)*

The Sixth Doctor Colin Baker had to endure freezing temperatures when he filmed his only Dalek story, *Revelation of the Daleks*, in the snow at Butser Hill near Petersfield. IBM's then futuristic looking UK headquarters at North Harbour, Portsmouth, was used for later scenes also shot in the snow. Blists Hill Victorian Town in Shropshire was used in The *Mark of the Rani*. Camber Sands in East Sussex was used for *The Ultimate Foe* (and had also been used for *The Chase* and the films *Dunkirk* and *Carry On: Follow That Camel*).

The Seventh Doctor - Sylvester McCoy *(1987-1989)*

The Seventh Doctor Sylvester McCoy was supposed to film his 1988 story Silver Nemesis at Windsor Castle, but this was blocked by officials so the shoot was switched to Arundel Castle in West Sussex which played Windsor instead. In later scenes Greenwich Gas Works was used as a landing site for a Cyberfleet. Lulworth Cove in Dorset featured in *The Curse of Fenric* and Kew Bridge Steam Museum in Brentford (see www.kbsm.org) was used in *Remembrance of the Daleks*.

The Eighth Doctor – Paul McGann *(1996)*

Paul McGann made just one appearance as the eighth Doctor in the 1996 adventure *Enemy Within* which was filmed in Canada and San Francisco.

Edge of Darkness
Manod

The '80s BBC thriller *Edge of Darkness* saw the late Bob Peck play Yorkshire detective Ronald Craven who was investigating the death of his daughter Emma who'd been part of an ecology group which had discovered a secret nuclear plant Northmoor under the Welsh mountains. In reality Northmoor was created by set designers who built an underground complex inside a disused slate mine at Manod, Blaenau Ffestiniog. The entrance used by Craven and CIA officer Darius Jedburgh to enter Northmoor was actually shot at a gold mine at Dolgellau. Llechwedd Slate Caverns at Blaenau Ffestiniog are open to the public. For details telephone 01766 830306 or visit www.llechwedd-slate-caverns.co.uk The conference sequence in the last episode was filmed at Gleneagles in Scotland.

Above: The Cavern at Llechwedd Slate Caverns.

Sat nav references:

Llechwedd Slate Caverns (LL41 3NB)

Gavin and Stacey
Barry

The gentle comedy series *Gavin and Stacey* won millions of fans and rightly garnered a string of awards. It has also done much to put the Welsh town of Barry, a few miles from Cardiff, on the map. In the show, which ran from 2007 to 2010, Stacey (Joanna Page) was from Barry and Gavin (Matthew Horne) was from Essex. But the difference in backgrounds and culture didn't hinder their romance which flourished when they finally met after hitting it off during numerous flirtatious work calls.

Despite being supposedly set in Barry and Essex, location filming for the show was all done in and around Barry, a small town in the Vale of Glamorgan, South Wales. Stacey's house was a private residence on Trinity Street and Gavin's parents' home, supposedly in Billericay, Essex, was in Dinas Powys, the next settlement to Barry. Gavin and his mate Neil's (James Corden) local pub in Essex was actually the Colcot Arms, Colcot Road, Barry. The amusement arcade where Nessa (Ruth Jones) worked was at The Western Shelter, Barry Island, Barry's coastal resort and when the family went on a bingo outing during series two those scenes were filmed at Penarth Pier. King's Square in the centre of Barry, outside the Town Hall, was the spot where Nessa decided to try to earn some money as a performance artist. Also featured regularly was Barry Town Station and the branch of Burger King where Gavin's sister worked, again supposedly in Essex, was at Culverhouse Cross near Barry.

Sat nav references:

Colcot Arms (CF62 8UJ)
Dinas Powys (CF64 4TH)
Town Station (CF62 8AF)
Trinity Street (CF62 7EW)
The Western Shelter (CF62 5TQ)

Our Mutual Friend

The Blitz, combined with modern development, caused a headache for the production team preparing to recreate 1860s London for the BBC's 1998 version of *Our Mutual Friend* which starred Paul McGann, Anna Friel, David Morrissey and Keeley Hawes. The major location was a sprawling warehouse on the riverfront overlooking the Thames at Southwark, but there was no genuine site which fitted the bill so a set was built at Cardiff Docks. Elsewhere, a disused stone quarry at Trifil, Wales was used and 17th Century Honington Hall, Shipston-on-Stour, Warwickshire played Mr and Mrs Boffin's home after they gained their wealth. Scenes were also filmed all over London including the English Speaking Union in Charles Street, which played the Veneering's house, the Middle Temple, Lincoln's Inn Fields, Gun Street and Somerset House. The back streets scenes behind the warehouses were filmed at Chatham Historic Dockyard.

Sat nav references:

Chatham Historic Dockyard (ME4 4TE)
English Speaking Union (W1J 5ED)
Honington Hall (CV36 5AA)

The Prisoner
Portmeirion

The cult 1960s series *The Prisoner* was filmed at the privately owned Mediterranean-style village of Portmeirion in North Wales. The village, situated at the top of a wooded clifftop, on its own private peninsula overlooking the Traeth Bach estuary and Cardigan Bay, was the inspiration of architect Sir Clough Williams-Ellis who fell in love with the Italian fishing village of Portofino as a young man and resolved to one day create something as charming in Britain. In

Above: It looks like it could be Italy, but actually it's Portmeirion in Wales.

Above: Three views of Sir Clough Williams-Ellis' amazing creation, Portmeirion.

1925 he bought a small craggy, wooded peninsula situated between Harlech and Porthmadog. Over the next few years he converted an early Victorian house on the site into a luxury hotel and added cottages. He travelled the country purchasing architecturally interesting but dilapidated buildings, set for demolition, which he brought to Portmeirion and rebuilt.

The village, which became a popular place for visitors including Edward VIII, HG Wells, John Steinbeck and Noel Coward, who wrote his play *Blithe Spirit* while staying at the hotel, was completed in 1973 and now comprises 50 buildings arranged around a central piazza. Actor Patrick McGoohan discovered Portmeirion while filming an episode of his 60s spy series *Danger Man* in Wales. He realised it was the perfect location for a new series he'd been planning called *The Prisoner*, which showbiz mogul Lew Grade had agreed to finance with a then unheard-of budget of £75,000 an episode.

The series followed the surreal adventures of an ex-spy with no name, just a number - Number Six - marooned in a strange village from which he constantly tried to escape. The 17-part series was a massive hit attracting around 12 million viewers each week. Today the series enjoys cult status and members of The Prisoner Appreciation Society, Six of One, stage a yearly convention at Portmeirion where they re-enact episodes and play the famous Human Chess Game. Portmeirion is open all year round. The hotel was gutted by fire in 1981, but has now been completely renovated and is a splendid place to stay. It has also become a popular venue for weddings. For further information see www.portmeirion-village.com.

Sat nav references:

Portmeirion (LL48 6ER)

Sherlock
Cardiff

Following the huge success of *Doctor Who*, Wales has become a firm favourite for filming and much of this successful series is shot in Cardiff and other parts of South Wales including Swansea and Merthyr Tydfil. Cities and towns within easy reach such as Bristol have also appeared in some episodes and some scenes were filmed in London.

Sherlock is a BBC Wales and Hartswood Films production, co-created by the proven partnership of Steven Moffat and Mark Gatiss and produced by Hartswood's Sue Vertue. It sees the classic Sherlock Holmes tale recreated with a modern and amusing take with actors Benedict Cumberbatch and Martin Freeman, in the roles of sleuths Sherlock Holmes and his sidekick Dr John Watson.

Soon after *Sherlock* made its debut in 2010, some of the filming locations featured became popular tourist attractions with viewers recognising them almost immediately they appeared on screen. For instance, the No Sign Bar in Wind Street, Swansea (www.nosignbar.co.uk) suddenly became busier than ever, despite the fact it was skillfully disguised onscreen as Angelo's, an Italian restaurant where Holmes and Watson ate in the pilot. Scenes were also shot outside the bar and at one point bemused passers-by had to be politely moved along as the night shoot threatened to

Above: **Benedict Cumberbatch** runs through the streets of Cardiff while filming a scene from *Sherlock*.

be disrupted. Nearby, Green Dragon Lane off Wind Street was redesigned into a Westminster street complete with W1 street signs. The road is cobbled and doubled up successfully as a London road.

While *Sherlock* is filmed at Upper Boat studios in Cardiff, a major part of each series tends to be shot on location. For example, in series one, St Bartholomew's, England's oldest hospital and known fondly as St Bart's, featured in all three episodes. (It was the site of the first meeting between Holmes and Watson both onscreen and in Conan Doyle's original stories.) Although the interiors of the hospital labs where the pair met were actually shot at a real laboratory within Cardiff University, the exterior of St Bart's and the rooftop were used in *Sherlock*. The production returned to St Bart's to shoot episodes one and three of series two. Fans will recall the dramatic finale to the second series, *The Reichenbach Fall* in which Holmes was seen plunging to his 'death' only to be seen alive moments later. This was shot on the rooftop of St Bart's to which there is no public access.

Not surprisingly then, the first episode of *Sherlock* series three, *The Empty Hearse*, returned to the hospital so Holmes's fake mystery death could be explained. The iconic 221B Baker Street is filmed in London, although round the corner at North Gower Street, W1. The real Baker Street couldn't be used as apart from being extremely busy, there are too many references to Sherlock Holmes which would have to be disguised.

As *Sherlock* is a modern version of the classic, there were discussions as to whether to include the number 221B on Holmes' front door as today there would be doorbells for each flat. In the end it was decided that the sign is too well known to alter so 221B it is. While shooting the pilot and series one and two of *Sherlock*, the flat door was removed and replaced with a door bearing the number 221B and then swapped back. But after filming of the second series ended, it was left as it is which made it handy for filming series three.

The actual number of the flat used is 187 which can be found to the left of a small sandwich shop called Speedy's. (In the pilot it was renamed Mrs Hudson's Snax but this has since been changed back to Speedy's and appears on screen as such.)

The café found instant fame as soon as it appeared on screen and attracted hundreds of new customers just weeks after the pilot of *Sherlock* hit BBC1. Most shots used were exterior but in the episode *A Scandal in Belgravia* in series two, the inside of Speedy's was used. The art department repainted the café which the owners were very happy about!

Other London locations which have appeared in *Sherlock* include Russell Square Gardens which is a 10-minute walk from North Gower Road and where Watson bumped into his old friend Mike Stanford in *A Study in Pink*. Trafalgar Square has cropped up in more than one episode as has New Scotland Yard.

Closer to the studios, Cardiff University proved useful as already mentioned with the stairs and corridors of the Main Building heavily featured in series two.

In the episode *The Blind Banker* the National Museum of Wales in Cardiff doubled up as the National Antiquities Museum. Streets used included Newport Road in Cardiff as well as roads in Merthyr Tydfil, all obviously picked to look like London.

For the first time, Cheltenham in Gloucestershire was used as a *Sherlock* filming location, in series three when The Daffodil restaurant, a converted 1920s picture house appeared in the first episode.

Nearby Bristol featured heavily in the second episode, *Sign of Three* with St Mary's Church in Sneyd Park the venue for the wedding of John Watson and Mary Morstan, played by his real-life partner Amanda Abbington. The reception scenes were shot in the Orangery at Goldney Hall, part of Bristol University. Spectacular mansion Swinhay House in Gloucestershire featured as the futuristic home of the master blackmailer in the series finale, *His Last Vow*.

Sat nav references:

Cardiff University's Main Building (CF10 3AT)
Daffodil (GL50 2AE)
National Museum of Wales (CF10 3NP)
No Sign Bar (SA1 1EG)
Speedy's (NW1 2NJ)
St Bart's Hospital (EC1A 7BE)

The North West

Bread
Brookside
Coronation Street
Last Tango in Halifax

Life on Mars
Pride and Prejudice
The Village

Bread
Liverpool

Elswick Street used to be just another smart row of two-up, two-down terraced houses a few yards from the River Mersey in Liverpool. But all that changed when a BBC film crew arrived in 1986 - and it ended up becoming one of the most famous streets in Britain. As the setting for the comedy series *Bread*, Elswick Street became a popular place for tourists to visit. The big Boswell family lived at Number 30 on screen

Above: Elswick Street in Liverpool, the setting for *Bread*.

and grumpy Grandad lived next door at Number 28. Bread's writer Carla Lane chose Elswick Street to appear in *Bread* because it fitted the image she had of where the Boswells lived and because the road ran down to the River Mersey it suited the scenes she planned to write. When she writes a script Carla said she actually tells the location manager on the show where she thinks something should be filmed. "I go out on my own and look at places and then I write them in a script," she revealed. "Then the BBC go out and find them from there. I give them more than a hint - I tell them where!"

Brookside
Liverpool

In the world of television soaps a great deal of time is spent making sets look just like the real thing. *Coronation Street*, although it looks just like a typical Manchester Street, isn't genuine and the houses in Albert Square, home of *EastEnders*, are fake and don't have backs to them.

Brookside, which ran from 1982 to 2003, was different - the houses seen on screen in the Merseyside soap are very real and were in Brookside Close, a cul-de-sac off Deysbrook

Above: The Brookside estate.

Lane on a real estate in the West Derby area of Liverpool. The houses were bought for the programme by *Brookside* creator Phil Redmond and were separated from actual homes nearby by a security barrier.

When characters went through an alleyway between Brookside Close and arrived at Brookside Parade shops it looked as if they'd just walked a few yards. It was just a clever illusion as in actual fact the Brookside Parade, offices and other scenes were filmed five miles away on the site of a former further education college at Childwall.

After filming ended, the 13 houses in the close – six used on screen and seven for production – were left empty until they were bought and restored by a local property developer. He then advertised for Brookside Close homes to rent and currently has tenants happily living in one of the most well-known cul-de-sacs in the country.

Coronation Street
Manchester

Britain's longest-running soap first aired in 1960 and in 2010 celebrated an incredible 50 years with a dramatic live episode and a tram crash causing devastation to the Street and its residents. Set in fictional Weatherfield, *Coronation Street*, or *Corrie* as it is fondly known, is shot mainly on a set at Granada Television's studios in Manchester, although outside locations are also used from time to time. The original Corrie outside set was built in 1969. Until that point, everything had been filmed inside a studio. That set was demolished in 1982 and the current one situated in Quay Street was built at the same time. It was officially opened by The Queen.

The soap's sets change and evolve to meet the needs of the storylines as well as technology. The first sets back

Above: An aerial view of the new *Coronation Street* studios under construction

in the '60s were long and thin because of fixed lens cameras. Now they can be designed as required; it's simply up to the designers' brief and imagination. As fans of the drama will know, the set incorporates regular fixtures: the Rover's Return pub which was burnt down and refurbished in 2013, a corner shop, a row of terraced houses, two shop units, three houses and a factory – all built in the '80s. Since then, other features have been added from time to time, such as Leanne Battersby's (now Tilsey) Italian restaurant which later burnt down, a bar opened by Leanne and Nick Tilsey which unfortunately blew up in the tram crash but is now the successful Bistro, a betting shop which was updated in 2013 and Audrey's hair salon, to name a few.

In 1988 the Granada Studios Tour was opened to the public and millions had the opportunity to walk down the famous cobbles of Coronation Street. They were able to stand at the bar in the Rover's Return and peek into Rita's sweet shop, the Kabin, which later became a victim of the tram crash. (The Kabin is now owned by Norris Cole although Rita works there still.)

Unfortunately Granada stopped offering tours in 1999. Some of the off-set locations used by *Corrie* over the years include the stunning Arley Hall and Gardens Estate near Northwich. Open to the public for corporate events and weddings, it has served as an ideal venue for a number of *Coronation Street* weddings. For instance, Maria Sutherland and the late Liam Connor tied the knot there as did Steve McDonald and Karen Philips. For further information, go to www.arleyhallandgardens. com.

Sarah Platt and Jason Grimshaw picked the attractive Ryecroft Hall in Ashton for their wedding. The Hall, a grade II listed building used as a community centre, has been used many times as Weatherfield Register Office including for the weddings of Steve and Becky and Gail and Joe, while other *Corrie* weddings and funerals have been filmed at a church in Prestwich.

Richard Hillman met a watery death in 2003 after driving himself and his family into a canal. This was

Above: One of the most recognisable sights in Britain...*Coronation Street.*

shot at the Portland Basin Museum, Portland Place, Ashton-under-Lyne. Other regularly used external locations include Victoria Railway Station, Salford, Manchester's Victoria Station, St Antony's Centre in Trafford is used as Weatherfield Community Centre and Europe's biggest municipal park, Heaton Park, has appeared many times.

In 2013 the filming of *Coronation Street* transferred to a new replica set Salford Quays, home to the MediaCity UK. The set and studios are situated next to the Imperial War Museum North are linked by a new bridge across the Manchester Ship Canal to the rest of the complex, which is home to a large BBC studios. The new 7.7-acre Coronation Street production centre includes two soundstage buildings, specialist production facilities, offices, dressing rooms and meeting space for production staff. One of the main advantages is that the familiar sets – including the refurbished Rovers Return - are now replicated slightly larger so camera crews and actors have greater flexibility. If viewers looked closely enough when the Rovers' reopening party scene was screened in May 2013 they may have noticed that while the décor remained the same, the pub was actually 'bigger' and cleverly had a few more nooks and crannies.

Sat nav references:

Arley Hall (CW9 6NA)
MediaCity UK (M50 2EQ)
Portland Basin Museum (OL7 0QA)
Ryecroft Hall (M34 5ZJ)

Last Tango in Halifax
Rochdale

Judging by the title, one could be forgiven for expecting this series to be shot entirely – or certainly mostly – on location in Yorkshire. However, due to various production constraints, most of the programme was filmed nearer to Manchester as this is where Red Production Company, which makes *Last Tango in Halifax*, is based.

Above: Anne Reid as Celia and Sir Derek Jacobi as Alan in a scene from *Last Tango in Halifax*.

The rural farm, complete with spectacular views and home to central character Alan Buttershaw (Derek Jacobi) and his daughter Gillian is supposedly in Halifax but is actually in Rochdale, Lancashire. The privately-owned working farm is part of the Manor of Rochdale and real-life home to a farmer who has enjoyed rearing sheep for many years. He's only too happy to have the production crew move in for a few weeks at a time to shoot exteriors at the property, especially as they have very little to change for filming purposes. The interior of the farmhouse is a specially-constructed set.

"I have to say, when *Last Tango* went out I was paying attention to what people were saying about it on Twitter," said location manager Andy Morgan. "One or two people pointed out, 'That's not Yorkshire' and I said, 'True!' It comes as a great shock to people when they discover places are not where they think they're supposed to be. As I point out, the story's set in Halifax but it doesn't mean we have to film there. As long as it looks like Halifax, that's what matters!"

Fans of the show may recall a beautiful stately home in which the happy couple, Alan and Celia considered it as a wedding venue in series one and ended up getting locked in overnight. The building in question was given the fictional name of Southowram Hall on screen but is in fact Bramall Hall in Stockport. This magical Tudor mansion is set in 60 acres of stunning parkland and is open to the public. For more details, go to www.bramallhall.org.uk or telephone 0161 4853708. The picturesque Pack Horse Inn pub at Birtle also made an appearance in the series, as did the Co-op supermarket in Marsden, which played the shop in which Gillian worked.

A lot of the picturesque scenery which makes *Last Tango* so watchable - the feel-good drama attracted six and a half million viewers when it first aired, making it BBC1's highest-rated launch of any show in 2012 - is filmed largely around Saddleworth Moor, at the crux of Greater Manchester, Calderdale

Right: (top) **Sarah Lancashire as Caroline,** *(middle)* **Policeman Robbie (Dean Andrews) right at the farm with Raff (Josh Bolt), William (Edward Ashley) and Louis Greatorex (Lawrence)** and *(bottom)* **Anne Reid and Sir Derek Jacobi.**

Above: Gillian (Nicola Walker), Raff (Josh Bolt) and Sarah Lancashire as Caroline.
Below: Anne Reid as Celia, Sir Derek Jacobi as Alan, Nicola Walker as Gillian and Sarah Lancashire as Caroline.

and West Yorkshire. One road goes through three different areas. Thanks to a great deal of clever shooting, several areas are often linked together in one sequence – something even the most discerning viewer probably wouldn't notice.

For instance, in series one, the car chase sequence which occurred on Celia and Alan's first date was actually shot in five separate locations and edited to make it look like just one. They both parked their cars in different car parks in Hebden Bridge. They then met for coffee in a café in Knutsford. The car chase ensued shortly afterwards down Skipton High Street and they finally crashed in the market square in Stockport, having already been seen chasing through the landscape outside Skipton. "It's not just a whim which makes us use several locations for one sequence, there are very good logistical and financial reasons for the way we film," explained Andy.

Other points of interest include the large, impressive school where Caroline is Headmistress. It's supposed to be in Harrogate but is actually the leading independent Bolton School in Bolton. And the opening scene of the first episode showed the characters in Betty's Tea Room in Harrogate but was actually filmed at Manchester Town Hall Café. Unfortunately, the beautiful family house where Caroline lives with her boys and estranged husband is privately owned and therefore out of bounds to the public. The pale brick property was supposed to be in Harrogate in the drama but in reality is in Bowden, Cheshire and was stumbled upon by Andy Morgan while location scouting. Series two was broadcast in autumn 2013, ending on Christmas Eve with the wedding celebrations of Celia and Alan. Stunning Jacobean Holdsworth House in Calderdale near Halifax was used as the restaurant and exterior of the reception venue while the interiors were shot at Hoghton Tower near Preston.

Sat nav references:

Bolton School (BL1 4PA)
Bramhall Hall (SK7 3NX)
Manchester Town Hall Café (M60 2LA)
Pack Horse Inn (BL9 7TU)

Life on Mars
Stockport

The first series of *Life on Mars* was screened by the BBC in 2006 and became an instant hit with viewers, going on to win both an Emmy and a BAFTA. Thanks to its quirky storyline and top notch cast – notably John Simm and Philip Glennister – it quickly developed a cult following which has remained loyal, despite only one more series being made the following year. It told the story of DCI Sam Tyler, played by Simm, an officer with the Greater Manchester Police who woke up in 1973 after being hit by a car. He found himself working for Manchester and Salford police force as a DI with a new boss, the maverick DCI Gene Hunt (Glenister).

Described as a 'science-fiction cop drama,' viewers were left wondering whether Tyler was dreaming his new life or whether he really had travelled back in time. Originally, the series was going to be shot in London which then changed to Leeds. Two months before filming began it was settled – Manchester was the chosen location. Tuning in every week while the show was still on air, it was fun for locals to try to recognise various landmarks in and around Manchester, Bury, Oldham, Salford and Stockport and there are still websites dedicated to location spotting.

Right: John Simm as Sam Tyler and Philip Glenister as DCI Gene Hunt in *Life on Mars*.

The police station used by the A Division CID team was actually the back of Stopford House, the home of Stockport Council Offices on Piccadilly. With its close proximity to the M60, the A6 and the centre of Manchester it made sense that it was chosen by the location team to double as the now iconic cop shop so closely associated with *Life on Mars*. Behind the council building is Stopford Piazza which also featured heavily in the show revamped as a 70's police station car park, complete with Cortinas, bicycles and lampposts. Most of the interior scenes such as the main CID office were shot on a purpose-built set at the BBC's studios in Manchester.

The spot where modern day Sam was hit by a car in the first episode was filmed in a service road underneath the Mancunian Way in Manchester, just off the A6 London Road heading towards Stockport.

The other two main places frequently revisited in *Life on Mars* were Sam's dingy home and the pub, both of which

Above: (top) Philip Glenister, Liz White and John Simm in a break during filming of *Life on Mars, (left)* John Simm as Sam Tyler.
Opposite: (top) Marshall Lancaster (DC Chris Skelton), Liz White (WPC Annie Cartwright) and Philip Glenister (DCI Gene Hunt) on location, *(opposite)* The scene of Sam's accident.

were specially created sets, but fans have always been quick to recognise a whole host of other locations which proved vital to the success of the show.

Many scenes were shot at the Rochdale Canal at Ancoats. The Grade II listed Victoria Baths in Hathersage Road, Manchester were used for at least two episodes. The 100-year-old building that houses both baths was used by the public until 1993 and is renowned for its exquisite architecture, stained glass and ornate tiling. The Turkish Baths within the same complex doubled as the morgue in series two while a real morgue at St Thomas's Hospital in Stockport was used as a morgue in series one.

Sat nav references:

Museum (BB10 2HX)
St Thomas's Hospital, Stockport (SK3 8BL)
Stockport Council Offices (SK1 3XE)
Victoria Baths (M13 0FE)

Pride and Prejudice
Disley

Jane Austen's comedy of manners *Pride and Prejudice* caused a sensation when it was screened on the BBC in September and October 1995 and turned its two lead actors Colin Firth, who played Mr Darcy, and Jennifer Ehle, who played Elizabeth Bennet, into stars. The story centres on Mrs Bennet, played by Alison Steadman, and her pursuit of husbands for her five daughters from the eligible rich young men who come into their social world in 19th Century Hertfordshire.

The BBC's previous version, adapted by Fay Weldon and screened in 1980, had been studio based but the six-part 1995 adaptation, written by award-winning screenwriter Andrew Davies, featured some of Britain's most stunning houses and countryside. For the purposes of filming, Mr Darcy's magnificent home Pemberley was quite a distance from Derbyshire, where it was supposed to be, and its exterior was actually filmed at beautiful Lyme Park near Stockport in Cheshire.

Lyme Park, one of the largest houses in the county, is owned by The National Trust and was the home of the Legh family for 600 years. Interior shots of Pemberley were actually filmed closer to where they were set, at late 17th Century

Above: Stunning Lyme Park, one of the largest stately homes in Britain was the main location for *Pride and Prejudice*.

Sudbury Hall in Derbyshire, which is again owned by The National Trust. Go to www.nationaltrust.org.uk for details.

The Bennet family home Longbourn was actually Luckington Court near Chipping Sodbury in Wiltshire. The house is privately owned and is a popular wedding reception venue but is not otherwise open to the public. For further details go to www.luckingtoncourt.co.uk

Just 15 miles away is the beautiful village of Lacock, which is also owned by The National Trust, and played Meryton on screen. The village dates back to the 13th Century and its lime washed half-timbered and stone houses also featured in *Harry Potter*, the ITV dramatisations of *Moll Flanders* and *Emma* and the BBC's *Cranford*.

The Ballroom at Brocket Hall, at Welwyn, Hertfordshire, was used for the main ball held at Netherfield. The Ballroom at Brocket Hall is now an upmarket conference venue. For details go to the Brocket Hall website at www.brocket-hall.co.uk The other scenes at Netherfield were filmed at Edgcote Hall near Banbury in Oxfordshire but this is privately owned and not open to the public. Rosings, home of Lady Catherine was played by Belton House at Grantham, Lincolnshire.

Belton, which was built in the late 17th Century, is also now owned by The National Trust and is open for much of the year. For further details go to www.national-trust.org.uk

Other scenes were filmed outside the Lord Leycester Hospital in Warwick and the Lambton

Above: Colin Firth and Jennifer Ehle as Mr Darcy and Elizabeth Bennet in the 1995 BBC adaptation of *Pride and Prejudice*.

Inn was in Chapel Street, Longnor, Staffordshire. Jane Austen's real house is now a museum and is located in the village of Chawton near Alton in Hampshire. For details see www.jane-austens-house-museum.org.uk The writer's grave can be found in Winchester Cathedral.

In 2013 PD James' novel, *Death Come to Pemberly*, was adapted for the BBC. It brought Jane Austen's characters to life once more but in a very different way. In the story Elizabeth and Darcy have been married for six years and have two young sons and as they prepare for the lavish annual ball at Pemberley, proceedings are interrupted by the unannounced arrival of Elizabeth's wayward sister Lydia, who stumbles out of her chaise screaming that her husband Wickham has been murdered...

Much of the drama, which starred Matthew Rhys as Darcy and Anna Maxwell Martin as Elizabeth, was filmed at one of Britain's finest stately homes, Chatsworth in Bakewell, Derbyshire. www.chatsworth.org Chatsworth, which has itself been the subject of its own documentary series, was used as the exterior of Pemberley, with Castle Howard near York (see Brideshead Revisited section) and Harewood House near Leeds (www.harewood.org) used for interior scenes.

Sat nav references:

Belton House at Grantham (NG32 2LS)
Brocket Hall (AL8 7XG)
Edgcote Hall (OX17 1AG)
Jane Austen's house (GU34 1SD)
Lord Leycester Hospital (CV34 4BH)
Luckington Court (SN14 6PG)
Lyme Park in Cheshire (SK12 2NR)
Winchester Cathedral (SO23 9LS)

The Village
Hayfield

The spectacular landscape of the Peak District was one of the real stars of this epic six-part BBC drama, which made its debut in 2013. With John Simm and Maxine Peake heading a stellar cast, *The Village* captured the story of a typical English village through the 20th Century. Largely told through the eyes of a man called Bert Middleton, it began with the often harsh and turbulent early years in the run up to and just after World War One.

Above: **Hayfield, the stunning location for *The Village*.**

The village of Hayfield, ten miles north of the spa town of Buxton, was the main location used for filming and from September until December 2012 the production team moved into the north Derbyshire village to create the fictional version, along with some surrounding areas including Glossop, Chapel-en-le Frith and Edale. Hayfield has strong connections to television as it was the birthplace and childhood home of actor Arthur Lowe, who played Captain Mainwaring in *Dad's Army*, and the Lantern Pike Inn in nearby Little Hayfield was where *Coronation Street* creator Tony Warren wrote the first episodes of the soap back in 1960.

Not surprisingly, the residents of Hayfield were delighted to learn their beautiful village was to be the focus of this ambitious production and were only too happy to accommodate the cast and crew. The production

held a casting for extras and some lucky locals found themselves on prime time television. Many real-life stores doubled up as fictional stores in the series including Derbyshire's fruit and veg shop on Kinder Road which became Hankins on screen. The owners liked the name so much they have kept it which will come in handy as the BBC has confirmed a new series of *The Village* is to be filmed once again in Hayfield. Nearby Rosie's Tea & Coffee Room became the exterior of a drapery shop. While the premises itself were not used for shooting, the owners Deidre and Andrew Stables (Rosie is their daughter) were happy to welcome in cast and crew for many a cuppa during the course of filming.

"We were a bit concerned initially that filming could lose us business as they had to close off the road," explained Andrew. "But the BBC assured us if we did, they would compensate us. We did lose some customers as cyclists couldn't get through but then we gained with the extra tourists who came to see the filming so it balanced itself out."

Other familiar buildings featured in *The Village* include the vicarage which served as the doctor's surgery and the Royal Hotel which was featured as the exterior of the village pub, The Lamb. The production also used the hotel as a base for the actors and set up hair and make-up in some of the rooms.

Situated in the heart of Hayfield next to the cricket club and by the River Sett, the hotel is an 18th Century coaching inn and an ideal base from which to explore the Peak District. Go to www. theroyalhayfield.co.uk for details.

Left: The clock was turned back on Hayfield for filming of *The Village*. *Opposite:* Maxine Peake and Nico Mirallegro shooting a scene as Grace and Joe Middleton.

Close to Rosie's, a cobbled walkway leads to The Royal Hotel and this frequently popped up in the drama. A fake entrance to the fictional Lamb was erected on the path, although the interiors of the pub were actually shot a few miles away in Chapel-en-le-Frith.

Hayfield Cricket Club's pitch also featured in *The Village* as a playing field. The white stone wall around the pitch was painted brown as it would have been at the turn of the 20th Century. And the village library doubled up as the public baths on screen.

Outside Hayfield, fields of privately owned Tattondale Farm in nearby Knutsford were used as fields belonging to both Middleton and Rutter, even though on screen the two owned farms opposite each other. And Highfield Farm, again a privately owned property, doubled up on screen as both the Middleton and Rutter farms.

When the drama's creator Peter Moffat visited the Middleton Farm up on Edale his first reaction was "that it was incredibly beautiful and at the same time very wild. Exactly as I'd imagined it. Then when I met the farmer Roy, who is in his 80s and was born there and has never left, fiction and historical reality joined up."

The village school was shot at the Old Duke of Norfolk Primary School in Glossop, which is a period building, as Hayfield's own school happens to be too modern to feature in the drama.

When Director Gillies MacKinnon saw the river in Hayfield he wanted to find a way to work it into the story. The desperation of John and Grace Middleton as they searched for Young Bert in episode five was the perfect opportunity to get a night shot of John Simm as John Middleton wading through the freezing water.

Right: (top) John Sim as John Middleton, *(middle and bottom)* Historic vehicles and set dressing help recreate a village from the past.

Sat nav references:

Hayfield Cricket Club (SK22 2PL)
Rosies Tea & Coffee Room (SK22 2HS)
The Royal Hotel (SK22 2EP)

The North

All Creatures Great and Small

Born and Bred

Brideshead Revisited

Emmerdale

Heartbeat

Jane Eyre

Last of the Summer Wine

Open All Hours

The Royal

South Riding

Vera

Wire in the Blood

All Creatures Great and Small
Askrigg

All Creatures Great and Small was one of the BBC's biggest drama hits of the '70s and '80s. Based on the novels of vet James Herriot, the series starred Christopher Timothy as Herriot and Robert Hardy as his partner Siegfried Farnon. The real-life surgery on which the books were based was in Thirsk, but the BBC used pretty Askrigg to play fictional Darrowby. Clearly visible in the village is tall Skeldale House which played the vets' surgery. Next door is Sykes Store, which played a sweet shop in the series and across is a building which was used as the grocer's shop. Nearby is The King's Arms, which played The Drover's Arms. Not far from Askrigg is Bolton Castle, where James proposed to Helen. It was also used in the BBC series *Ivanhoe* and the feature film *Elizabeth*. See www.boltoncastle.co.uk for more details. Other locations used in the series included: the market in Hawes, which played Darrowby Cattle Market, Hardraw church which was Darrowby church and Wensley church, where James and Helen were married.

Above: James Herriot (Christopher Timothy) and Siegfried Farnon (Robert Hardy) the stars of *All Creatures Great and Small*.

Sat nav references:

Bolton Castle (DL8 4ET)
The King's Arms (DL8 3HQ)
Wensley Church (DL8 4HX)

Born and Bred
Downham

Stunning scenery helped make *Born and Bred* compelling Sunday night viewing between 2002 and 2005. Set in the fictional Lancashire village of Ormston during the '50s, it centred on the relationship between village GP Arthur Gilder (James Bolam) and his city-trained doctor son Tom Gilder, played by Michael French. Much of the family drama was filmed in the real-life village of Downham, near Clitheroe in Lancashire. The village is privately-owned by Lord and Lady Clitheroe and every home is rented by the villagers. What makes it the perfect location for a '50s-set series such as this is the fact that certain trappings of modern day life are banned, making it not too dissimilar to the way it was centuries ago. Ormston Hospital was the exterior of three houses within the village.

Above: The pretty village of Downham played Ormston in the popular BBC series *Born and Bred*.

Sat nav references:

Downham (BB7 4BJ)

Brideshead Revisited
Castle Howard

When it was first screened in 1981 the worldwide success of the ITV epic drama *Brideshead Revisited* brought thousands of extra visitors flocking to the series' principal location, Castle Howard in Yorkshire. And even now, so many years later, it still contributes heavily to the number of visitors to Castle Howard, which has been the seat of the Howard family for more than three centuries. *Brideshead Revisited* is often cited as one

Above: Stunning Castle Howard, setting for *Brideshead Revisited.*

of ITV's biggest successes - both in terms of critical acclaim and ratings.

When the series went into production Granada managed to find a distinguished cast including Laurence Olivier, John Gielgud, Anthony Andrews and Jeremy Irons. The tale of love and passion during the inter-war years was filmed against a backdrop of 18th Century Castle Howard, one of the finest stately homes in Britain which is set in 1,000 acres of parkland and is as stunning on the outside as it is beautiful inside.

In 1994 the BBC returned to film the costume drama *The Buccaneers* and in the summer of 2007 a new version of *Brideshead Revisited* went into production starring Michael Gambon and Emma Thompson much of it was also filmed at Castle Howard. For more details and opening times see www.castlehoward.co.uk

Sat nav references:

Castle Howard (YO31 7QA)

Emmerdale
Esholt

There's good news and bad news for fans of the ITV soap *Emmerdale*, Britain's second longest-running soap after *Coronation Street*. First the good news: you can visit both villages originally used as the fictional Yorkshire village of Beckindale in the series. The bad news is that you can no longer visit the exterior locations for the show since filming was switched from the village of Esholt to a specially-built set on an estate in North Yorkshire in January 1998.

The pretty village of Arncliffe played the first Beckindale but production was moved in 1976 because producers decided to find somewhere closer to Leeds where the interior scenes are recorded, because it was quite a trek to Arncliffe. Not only that, Arncliffe had become a Mecca for

Above: It looks real - but the *Emmerdale* pictured here is a specially-built set.

fans and the village just couldn't cope. A local hotel called The Falcon doubled up as the fictional Woolpack Inn and fans would arrive in their droves, hoping to see their favourite characters in the bar. Filming was switched to Esholt, just a few miles north west of Leeds, and that in turn became a magnet for lovers of the show, so much so that a special parking site for coaches had to be built nearby. This time, the village pub – the Commercial Hotel - served as the Woolpack and has since retained its adopted name.

In 1997 Yorkshire Television decided to build a purpose-built set on the estate which surrounds historic Harewood House near Leeds and which was once used for the ITV series *Follyfoot*. The success of the series and the pressures of extra episodes made shooting at Esholt too difficult. It had been fine when they only made one episode a week but new episodes heavily increased the workload.

Above: (left) **The real Woolpack in Esholt,** *(centre)* **the entrance to the television set village,** *(right)* **the television Woolpack.**

The new set, which took four months to build, isn't an exact replica of Esholt and Yorkshire Television received quite a few letters when it was first seen on screen because some viewers noticed the change, despite the efforts of expert painters and carpenters.

Unfortunately the set isn't open to the public and a few years ago Yorkshire Television stopped its popular tours of interior sets that it used to run at its Leeds studios. A small consolation is that you can watch a live webcam of the location set. Go to www.itv.com/emmerdale/about/village-webcams.

Not every location is on the Harewood Estate set. Creskeld Hall, a privately owned Grade II listed country house at Arthington doubles as Home Farm and has seen plenty of drama over the years including Frank Tate's death, the murder of Tom King and Zoe blowing up part of the house. It is now the longest serving location on the programme and is currently home to Declan and Katie Macey, played by Jason Merrells and Sammy Winward. Although Creskeld Hall is private and not open to the public, its gardens are sometimes open for visitors under the National Gardens Scheme. See (www.ngs.org.uk) for details. Rudding Park Hotel (www.ruddingpark.co.uk) in Harrogate has often appeared in the drama for a range of scenes including spa visits and meals out.

The 'old' Emmerdale village, Esholt, is still worth a visit as apart from the 'Woolpack' pub in Main Street, there is the village hall which has featured extensively in the series. Just opposite the hall is St Paul's Church which plays Beckindale Church, where Matt married Dolly, Kathy married Jackie and Joe married twice in the show.

Sat nav references:

Creskeld Hall (LS21 1NT)
St Paul's Church (BD17 7RA)
Woolpack pub (BD17 7QZ)

Market scenes have been filmed in the nearby town of Otley, which plays Hotten in the series and other places that are used include: Almscliffe Crag, Brimham Rocks, Plumpton Rocks, Valley Gardens, Harrogate and Golden Acre Park, Leeds. In addition Wakefield, Leeds and Morley town halls are used for courtroom scenes.

Heartbeat
Goathland

When the residents of picturesque North Yorkshire village Goathland learned this '60s-set drama had been axed after 18 years, they went into shock. For not only had *Heartbeat* been a Sunday night telly favourite for so long but it kept a healthy stream of visitors coming to the village, so boosting its economy.

At the start of the series in 1992, former *EastEnders* actor Nick Berry played London police constable Nick Rowan who quit his inner city beat to take a job as a rural village bobby along with his doctor wife Kate, played by Niamh Cusack. Inevitably over the many years the series ran, members of the cast changed and latterly it was Joe Mason (Joe McFadden) who pounded the rural beat along with PC Don Weatherby (Rupert Ward-Lewis).

While numbers of *Heartbeat* fans who arrive in Goathland each year have inevitably fallen as new episodes are no longer being made, the former popularity of the show (and repeats) mean that it is still an exciting area which attracts tourists keen to visit the locations they've seen on screen. There's plenty to see in Goathland, for example when you drive through the village you reach a right-hand bend and the stone house on your right is Glendale House, which played Kate Rowan's surgery in the series. The house was built in 1875 by Edward Fuller Sewell, an uncle of Anna Sewell, author of the novel *Black Beauty*. It's a Victorian

Above: PC Rob Walker (Jonathan Kerrigan), district nurse Carol Cassidy (Lisa Kay) and PC Phil Bellamy (Mark Jordon).

Above: A view of picturesque Goathland.

stone-built residence and occupies a prime position in the centre of the picturesque village overlooking the common, where sheep graze right outside the garden gate. Its owners, Keith and Sandra Simmonds, offer reasonably priced bed and breakfast. For details see www.glendalehouse.co.uk

Over at Brow House Farm, the location for Claude Greengrass' farm, farmers John and Keith Jackson have opened up some of their fields as a campsite. The site was up and running before *Heartbeat* began but once the series was broadcast, tourists were keener than ever to stay. In fact at one point business was so good, the Jacksons gave over another field to campers to cope with the demand. Bookings can be made by telephoning 01947 896274.

Real life Goathland Garage appeared in the series as Scripp's Garage and across the road from it is The Goathland Hotel which played the local pub, The Aidensfield Arms. You'll also see the shops which featured in the series including

Above: (top) Glendale House, which was used as Kate Rowan's surgery and is now a B&B, *(above)* Members of the crew dress the set.

the real post office which played the post office in the show and Aidensfield Stores, run by Phil and Ros Hopkinson, which remained the same on the outside whether filming was taking place or not and still sells a range of *Heartbeat* merchandise. See www.aidensfieldstores.co.uk for further details.

The Goathland Primary School featured heavily in the show when Nick Rowan's second wife Jo Weston was in the series and in real life the school benefited from a donation from Yorkshire Television which helped kit the pupils out in new school uniforms. A private house, Brereton Cottage on Brereton Corner played the police house and also not open to the public is a farm which played Peggy Armstrong and David Stockwell's farm.

We didn't often see the exterior of the police station in later episodes, but in earlier ones, the former police station in Courthouse Street, Otley, about 75 miles from Goathland, was used. When *Heartbeat* began, most scenes — both interior and exterior - were filmed in Goathland but later most interior scenes were shot at a studio built inside a former mill near Leeds, which was once used as the studio for filming interiors for *Emmerdale*. Sets of Ashfordly Police Station, the doctor's surgery and the pub were built as it proved cheaper and easier to film interior scenes there.

Sat nav references:

Aidensfield Stores (YO22 5LX)
Brow House Farm (YO22 5NP)
Glendale House (YO22 5AN)
Goathland Hotel (YO22 5LY)
Goathland Primary School (YO22 5ND)

Jane Eyre
Bakewell

An all-star cast helped make BBC's 2006 glossy adaptation of Charlotte Bronte's *Jane Eyre* one of the most popular television remakes of this much-loved classic, winning both an Emmy and a BAFTA the following year.

Dovedale, the rocky National Trust land in the Derbyshire Dales, featured in the opening episode where Rochester and Jane initially met in the mist. Rochester's home, Thornfield, was in fact Haddon Hall, a stunning medieval castle in Bakewell, Derbyshire which is owned by Lord and Lady Edward Manners. Some of the scenes supposedly set at Thornfield were in fact shot at a studio miles away and at another building.

North Haddon Hall has featured in a number of other television shows and films including the BBC's *The Prince and the Pauper* and more recently, the movie remake of *Pride and Prejudice*, starring Keira Knightley and Matthew MacFadyen. In particularly dramatic scenes, Thornfield was

Above: Beautiful Dovedale in the Derbyshire Dales.
Below: Ilam Park, one of the settings for *Jane Eyre*.

seen burning through the night thanks to the use of special effects. During filming the local fire brigade received dozens of calls from worried locals who believed Haddon Hall was genuinely on fire. For further information go to www. haddonhall.co.uk If you're planning on visiting Bakewell, why not take in the village of Hathersage in Derbyshire which is just an eight mile drive north. Once renowned for its milling industries, the area is now the perfect place to walk and climb as it is overlooked by moors and gritstone edges, including the well-known Stanage Edge. Ruth Wilson's Jane was seen standing there in episode four.

Charlotte Bronte visited Hathersage in 1845 and took the name Eyre for her novel's heroine from the local family. It is believed that she based Thornfield, the house from where Mrs Rochester jumped from the roof to her death, on North Lees Hall, an Elizabethan manor house which is situated about a mile north of Hathersage. The BBC used the Hall as Thornfield (along with Haddon Hall as mentioned earlier). The property is now owned by the Peak District National Park Authority and is open to the public for one weekend in September. Telephone Yorkshire Bridge Inn Ltd for further information on 01433 651361.

If you stood on Carhead Rocks above North Lees Hall and looked behind you, you'd see Overstones Farm, which doubled as Rivers Cottage. Much of the early part of *Jane Eyre* took place at Lowood School and for this the BBC opted for Bolsover Castle which provided some of the school's interiors. Built in the 12th Century, it is now in the care of English Heritage. It also served as Jane's school during her early years when she was played by the actress Georgie Henley. The Riding House at Bolsover Castle was transformed into the school's dormitory. Wingfield Manor at South Wingfield, near Alfreton, Derbyshire was used as Thornfield after the great fire wreaked havoc. The building has remained unoccupied since 1772 and is now owned by English Heritage. To arrange to visit or learn more about its history see www.english-heritage.org.uk

Ilam Hall at Ashbourne, a 19th Century Victorian Gothic manor house, and its surrounding gardens are managed by the National Trust and are now used as a youth hostel, tea rooms and car park. The hall doubled up as the exterior of Lowood School. Situated in the village of Ilam, it is to be found between Buxton and Ashbourne. For more details about the house see www.nationaltrust.org.uk Another Trust property, Kedleston Hall, an 18th Century mansion north-west of Derby, features in the scene where Rochester meets his future wife Bertha. The mansion is renowned for its art treasures and one particular room, Caesar's Hall, was transformed into a Caribbean setting where a lavish dinner was staged.

Sat nav references:

Bolsover Castle (S44 6PR)
Haddon Hall (DE45 1LA)
Ilam Hall (DE6 2AZ)
Kedleston Hall (DE22 5JH)
Wingfield Manor (DE55 7NH)

Last of the Summer Wine
Holmfirth

Above: **Nora Batty** dishes out justice to Compo, Foggy and Clegg.

For more than 40 years Roy Clarke's gentle comedy *Last of the Summer Wine* has given the Yorkshire town of Holmfirth the sort of publicity that tourism industry chiefs can usually only dream of. The series ran from 1973 to 2010 and helped put the town firmly on the tourist map and showed off the full beauty of the Pennine countryside. Each year thousands of fans of the BBC comedy still flock to Holmfirth to see for themselves the real-life setting for the show.

If you are planning a visit, a good first port of call - particularly after a long drive - must be the cafe used as Sid's Cafe in the series, latterly run on-screen by Ivy. A former paint store for a nearby hardware shop, the cafe looks much the same off-screen as on. Local man Colin Frost ran the cafe with his wife Maggie for 15 years until 2006 when it was taken over by sisters Ailsa and Laura Booth. Colin now runs tours of filming locations. See www.sumerwine.tv for details.

No trip to Holmfirth is complete without taking a peek at Nora Batty's famous house. It is just a short walk from the cafe along Hollowgate. At the end of Hollowgate is a bridge and from it you can see Nora's house, Number 28 Scarfold and below is the door to Compo's flat, which now houses The Summerwine Exhibition, run by Sue and Chris Gardner. The couple also own The Wrinkled Stocking Tea Room next door at Number 30, another good place to take a break.

It is open for most of the year. Nora's house is now available as a holiday cottage. Businessman Neil Worthington bought the house a few years ago and planned to expand his graphic design and advertising business at Numbers 24 and 26 into it. But he changed his mind and decided to open the world-famous house for self-catering accommodation instead. For booking details see: www.nora-batty.co.uk The house even contains some Nora Batty props and as Neil's website says it is "A shrine to Nora Batty, fully furnished, as only Nora would approve. Tastefully decorated in keeping with the overall Nora Batty Experience." Neil said: "We're quite unique – there aren't many film sets you can actually stay in."

While in the area you might like to call in for a pint at The White Horse Inn at Jackson Bridge which appeared in

Above: (left) **Nora Batty's famous steps,** *(centre)* **the iconic Sid's Cafe,** *(right)* **The White Horse at Jackson Bridge.**

Sat nav references:

The Butcher's Arms (HD9 1TE)
The Cafe (HD9 2DG)
The White Horse Inn (HD9 1LY)
The Wrinkled Stocking Tea Room (HD9 2JS)

the show many times. See www.thewhitehorsejacksonbridge.co.uk for details. Behind the pub at Jackson Bridge is the private house which doubled as home for Cleggy, Pearl and Howard. From Jackson Bridge you may like to drive to Hepworth where you'll find another of the trio's locals, The Butcher's Arms. See www.thebutchersarmshepworth.co.uk for details.

Open All Hours
Doncaster

You won't find Arkwright's grocers shop open all hours if you go to Number 15, Lister Avenue in Doncaster. Nor will you be able to buy a p-p-p-packet of cornflakes or a l-l-l-loaf of bread. But you might be able to get your hair cut! For the shop that played stuttering Arkwright's shop in the highly successful BBC comedy *Open All Hours*, and became Britain's best-known shop front between 1976 and 1985 is actually a hair salon.

The BBC picked the shop because it had a traditional double front and fitted the bill perfectly as Arkwright's old-style corner shop. So for three weeks a year, for four years, the BBC rolled their camera equipment into the street and moved owner Helen Ibbotson's hairdryers and curlers out of her shop. The BBC covered up Helen's Beautique sign with a board bearing Arkwright's name and dressed up the front of the shop with stocks of food. And, of course, they painted details of Arkwright's bargain of the week on the window.

Across the road from the shop is Number 34 which played the home of Arkwright's love, nurse Gladys Emmanuel (Lynda Baron). After it was used for the first series the then owner altered the look of the front of the house and when the BBC came to make the next series they decided it no longer suited them. So filming was switched to Number 32 next door - and the BBC hoped no one would notice. In 2006 Doncaster council chiefs put forward a new development plan for parts of the town which many people believed could see areas including Lister Avenue facing demolition. A petition and campaign have been set up against the plan, although councillors accused campaigners of scaremongering and said nothing had been finalised.

Above: (top) Ronnie Barker and David Jason as Arkwright and Granville on location in Doncaster, *(above)* the shop as it is now.

Sat nav references:

Hair Salon (DN4 8AS)

123

The Royal
Scarborough

When *Heartbeat* came to an end in 2010, sadly so did its spin-off *The Royal* which was filmed in the seaside town of Scarborough and centred around the fictional St Aiden's Royal Free Hospital. Exterior shots for the series, which starred Robert Daws as Dr Gordon Ormerod and Amy Robbins as Dr Jill Weatherill, were shot outside Red Court apartments in Holbeck Road. Interior scenes were filmed in a studio, but other locations that were used for the series include Goathland and Calverley.

South Riding
Yorkshire

Above: The beautiful scenery at Skipsea.

Andrew Davies's three-part adaptation of the novel by Winifred Holtby was screened by BBC One in February 2011 and was set against a stunning Yorkshire landscape. The story, set in the 1930s, saw the arrival from London to the South Riding, of career woman Sarah Burton (Anna Maxwell Martin) to take up the post of headmistress at a high school for girls.

Following the death of Sarah's fiancé in the First World War, she'd given up on marriage and motherhood but she hadn't banked on meeting Robert Carne (David Morrissey), a man whose family had farmed the South Riding for centuries and who had his own troubles...

The production was based in Leeds and interiors were shot in various areas across the region. For example, the interior of girls' school Kiplington High, was a disused infants' school on the outskirts of Leeds while the exterior was actually a completely different school – All Saints Primary in Bradford which looked similar.

"All the coastal locations used were at Skipsea, East Yorkshire," said location manager Luc Webster. "Because the site where the Shacks were was the original site (on which Holtby based her novel) we shot there. It was actually like a shanty town along the cliff tops. The Shacks were recreated on the disused Acaster Malbis Airfield, north Yorkshire (where the Holly family's railway carriage was also built) and the interior of the carriage was recreated at the studio in Leeds."

A large privately owned mansion house 10 miles outside Durham doubled up as Robert Carne's home while fans of the drama may be interested to learn that the character's stable yard actually formed part of another property, a stunning Grade II listed mansion called Rise Hall. The magnificent house belongs to television presenter Sarah Beeny and in fact her trials and tribulations in restoring it were featured on Channel Four's *Beeny's Restoration Nightmare*. It is now available for weddings and other events. Visit www.risehall.com to learn more.

The production crew found themselves on the road a good deal during the shoot and in fact travelled to an impressive 35 locations in 44 days. These included the seafront in Bridlington, a few areas in Harrogate and the Great Central Railway in Loughborough (www.gcrailway.co.uk). Many of the council scenes (and the Floral Hall concert) were filmed at Grade I listed Morley Town Hall at Morley near Leeds.

Sat nav references:

All Saints Primary (BD5 0NG)
Great Central Railway (LE11 1RW)
Morley Town Hall (LS27 9DY)
Rise Hall (HU11 5BL)

Vera
Northumberland

Above: **Brenda Blethyn as Detective Inspector Vera Stanhope on Tynemouth Pier.**

Stunning North East locations are the stars of ITV1's mystery crime drama *Vera*, along with actress Brenda Blethyn as DI Vera Stanhope. Filming takes place largely across beautiful Northumberland which boasts spectacular countryside and coastal stretches, showcased to full advantage in all the episodes. Northumberland County Council is thrilled with the popular drama as thanks to viewing figures averaging around seven million, it has given the region's tourist industry an almighty boost. And they are only too happy to give ITV Studios plenty of access to locations, roads and buildings to help make filming as easy as possible.

North Blyth, Druridge Bay, Low Hauxley, Embleton, Tod-le-Moor, Linhope Spout, Corbridge and Thrum Rocks are among the major areas used for shooting the episodes which are based on the work of successful North East writer Ann Cleeves. Key locations worth mentioning include the Headland in Hartlepool, an old area of the town which makes visitors feel as if they're stepping back in time. "It boasts fantastic old period housing and great colours, all sitting right on the sea," said location manager Andrew Bainbridge. "It's really an extraordinary place, very special."

Blast Beach which can be found just south of Seaham in County Durham was used in the third series of *Vera*, screened in April 2013. (The beach was also used in the movie *Get Carter*.) Dramatic and backed by high cliffs, the beach is covered in strikingly coloured rock, remnants of the coal dumping grounds and much of the sand is at times black with coal dust. Druridge Bay north of Blyth on the Northumberland Coast is a favourite filming location for the *Vera* production team with a seven-mile stretch of wonderful sands backed by huge dunes making it a particularly versatile place to film. "It's very beautiful but somehow very gritty too, real *Vera* territory," said Andrew. Chipchase Castle, a Grade I listed Jacobean stately home on the east bank of the North Tyne near Wark, Northumberland doubled up as the Cadvar Estate in series two. Set in classic *Vera* landscape, it is especially renowned for being particularly well-preserved and its gardens attract countless visitors. For information on opening hours go to www.chipchasecastle.com. Dunstanburgh Castle which featured in the very first episode, is also a must on any visitor's list. This magnificent ruin right on the north Northumberland coastline is run by English Heritage and boasts spectacular views. Go to www.english-heritage.org.uk for more details and opening times. Natural Retreats just above Richmond, north Yorkshire featured in episode two of series three of *Vera* and is an ideal place to consider if you're planning on discovering the Yorkshire Dales. This fabulous

Above: Stunning Dunstanburgh Castle.

self-catering holiday lodge park (www.naturalretreats.co.uk) is set in a beautiful location complete with comfortable contemporary lodges.

Another location worthy of note here can be found on the spectacular north Durham moors around Edmundbyers. The road running from Middleton in Teesdale up through Stanhope and onto Edmundbyers features heavily in many episodes of *Vera*. "It's like a moonscape up there and on a good day you can see for absolutely miles," Andrew promised. Other interesting locations viewers may want to visit having spotted them on screen, include the Rendezvous Café at Whitley Bay, an art deco café sitting right on the water just north of the town centre.

The Bridge Hotel, Newcastle which was featured in the final episode, sits directly beside the Moot Hall (the old law courts), the Vermont Hotel and the Castle Keep, also known as the Castle of Newcastle-Upon-Tyne and a major heritage site in the North East. Go to www.castlekeep-newcastle.org.uk to learn more about its history. For an idyllic and exciting family getaway, a forest adventure site, Go Ape! (www.goape.co.uk) close to Matfen Hall Hotel at Matfen, Northumberland is worth a look. It was used in episode three, series three. The Lit and Phil Library in Newcastle, a Grade II listed building which was opened in 1825 and welcomes members of the public featured in the same episode. It is said to be the most impressive library in the north of England and the largest independent library outside London. Go to www.litandphil.org.uk for further information. A fourth series of *Vera* began filming in the North East as series three was being screened, for broadcast in 2014.

Sat nav references:

Castle Keep (NE1 1RQ)
Chipchase Castle (NE8 3NT)
Dunstanburgh Castle (NE66 3TT)
Go Ape! (NE20 0RH)
The Lit and Phil Library (NE1 1SE)
Rendezvous Café (NE26 1TP)

Wire in the Blood
Newcastle

Above: The city of Newcastle was used as the setting for *Wire In The Blood*.

This gritty crime series was screened on ITV between 2002 and 2008, finally being axed in 2009 due to high production costs. Made by Coastal Productions, *Wire in the Blood* was filmed in and around Newcastle and starred Robson Green as clinical psychologist Dr Tony Hill who got inside the head of killers in order to help police solve bizarre crimes. He worked closely on a range of often gruesome cases with Detective Inspector Alex Fielding, played by Simone Lahbib, who took over in series four from Detective Chief Inspector Carol Jordan, played by Hermione Norris.

Newcastle itself was never mentioned in *Wire in the Blood*, which is supposedly based in the fictional metropolis of Bradfield. The storylines were generally dark and much of the show was filmed during the winter. A large part of *Wire in the Blood* was filmed on a purpose-built set, home to the police station, in Heaven, Newcastle. For the first three seasons, the inside of the police station was filmed in the former Bank of England in the centre of Newcastle. The building has an interesting history – it was the second biggest bullion store in the country outside of London – but the set itself wasn't felt to be especially interesting. The set used for the final season of *Wire in the Blood* began to take shape in series four when the production team came across a former Rolls Royce switch gear factory in the Team Valley. With its ranks of grey steel shelving and steel staircases, it was considered ideal police station material.

Unfortunately, after series four, the building wasn't available any longer so Gareth bought all of the steel staircases and grey shelving which were moved to another warehouse in Wallsend, Newcastle. The designer for series five remodelled the set using the props and made it even more camera-friendly. That was the blueprint for the set used for series six, although in the interim, the production lost the warehouse.

Sat nav references:

Bank of England (NE1 6SU)

Scotland

Balamory
Doctor Finlay
The Field of Blood
Hamish Macbeth
High Road

Monarch of the Glen
Shetland
Taggart
Waterloo Road

Balamory
Tobermory

Tobermory, the capital of the Isle of Mull, played host to this popular children's programme between 2002 and 2005. Screened on BBC1, BBC2 and CBeebies, the show was aimed at pre-schoolers and was set in the fictional small island community of Balamory.

Tobermory was considered the perfect location for the show thanks to its pretty, colourful houses which can be found on the harbour front and still attract plenty of interest from visitors. The programme centred around what happened in each house. It is important to point out that Josie Jump's house is a small hotel called Park Lodge which can be located a little distance away in a quieter part of the village. Go to www.park-lodge-tobermory.co.uk to make a booking. All the other houses used for filming are privately-owned but can be seen while passing.

All of the houses used in *Balamory* were in Tobermory which has served to put the Isle of Mull on the visitors' map. One exception was the North Berwick location for Archie's Castle which is now a successful hotel called Fenton Tower.

Sat nav references:

Fenton Tower (EH39 5JH)
Park Lodge (PA75 6PR)

An interesting and unique place to stay, Fenton Tower is a magnificent 16th Century tower which has been exquisitely refurbished to accommodate just 12 guests at a time. Go to www.fentontower.co.uk for further information.

Doctor Finlay
Auchtermuchty

Auchtermuchty became the fictional Scottish town of Tannochbrae in the 1993 series of *Doctor Finlay* by chance when producer Peter Wolfes drove through the town on his way to view another possible location. Many buildings in the town centre, The Cross, were used for filming and The Forest Hills Hotel became a temperance hotel, The Salvation. The Post Office appeared regularly although it was turned into The Flying Dutchman pub.

Auchtermuchty Town Hall, which was the town's police station many years ago and still has the old cells, reverted back to its former role to play Tannochbrae Police Station. The town's council offices doubled as the local bank and the entrance to the library was altered to fit the 1950's style and was used as Tannochbrae library. What was missing from

Sat nav references:

Auchtermuchty Town Hall (KY14 7AP)
The Forest Hills Hotel (KY14 7AP)
Post Office (KY14 7AR)

Auchtermuchty was the surgery, Arden House, and that was because it wasn't in the town. In fact it was more than 70 miles away on a country estate just outside Glasgow. The original 60s series *Doctor Finlay's Casebook* was filmed in Callander but producers decided not to use it for the 1993 series because it had become too busy.

The Field of Blood
Glasgow

The city of Glasgow provided the backdrop for BBC1 Scotland's award-winning period thriller *The Field of Blood* which was screened in 2010 and its follow up three years later, *The Field of Blood: The Dead Hour*.

Adapted from the novels of Denise Mina by writer and director David Kane, the stories were set in the cutthroat world of a Glasgow newspaper office in the early 1980s and an ambitious young woman's (Paddy Meehan played by BAFTA Scotland winner Jayd Johnson) determination to become an investigative reporter.

As location manager Michael Higson explained, Glasgow has a habit of reinventing itself every few decades so finding '80s-looking buildings at which to film proved tricky, although the team were ultimately successful. They managed to concentrate all scenes intended to be a number of different homes on one '80s housing estate. Most locations were required by the script to look hard and intimidating and while the housing estate used was in a quiet area, it had an 'edge' to it which worked well in the storyline.

Indeed, Michael's brief was to seek out 'creepy' and 'dark' locations in which to film around the Glasgow area. They were the kind of places where gangsters might hide kidnap victims for instance so often just small sections of venues were used to give the right feel. One such venue is the National Mining Museum in Midlothian which proved hugely atmospheric and intimidating whereas in reality, it is a top visitor attraction and based at one of the finest surviving examples of a Victorian colliery in Europe. Go to www.scottishminingmuseum.com for opening times and further information.

Another location worth a visit and one which was used in both series is Brechin's Bar which doubled up as the Press Bar on screen. Located in the heart of Govan and ninth on the Govan Heritage Trail, this period venue has also popped up in other TV dramas including *Rebus* and *Taggart*.

Sat nav references:

Brechin's Bar (G51 3DJ)
National Mining Museum (EH2 3PA)

Hamish Macbeth
Plockton

The sleepy village of Plockton on the north west coast of Scotland found fame in the late 1990s as the fictional village of Lochdubh, home beat of PC Hamish Macbeth, played by Robert Carlyle, who has gone on to become a major film star. To find the right location to play Lochdubh for the BBC series, the show's producers toured 1,200 miles of the west coast of Scotland.

Although remote, Plockton is just over the sea from Skye and attracts visitors from all over the world. It lies in a sheltered inlet, surrounded by heather-clad mountains and with views across Loch Carron. The gulf stream climate accounts for unexpected palm trees which fringe its harbour and seals are a common sight in its calm waters. Before the BBC team arrived en masse in the village Producer Deirdre Keir and her team made sure the locals were happy with the prospect of a 70-strong film unit arriving. Plockton's newsagent Edmund McKenzie agreed to move his shop into the sailing club next door for three months so that his premises could be used by the BBC and converted into the Lochdubh general store.

Visitors to Plockton were constantly surprised to find the village shop was faked and stocked only with props. The whitewashed house chosen to be both Hamish's home and the police station is a holiday home owned by a Glasgow doctor. On one occasion a family from London who had pre-booked a week's holiday arrived to find their cottage adorned with a blue lamp, bars at the windows and a police cell where a bedroom used to be.

High Road
Luss

The Scottish soap, which ran from 1980 to 2003, was filmed in Luss on the banks of Loch Lomond where the pretty village doubled as fictional Glendarroch. The big house in the series was actually the Youth Hostel at nearby Arden, which can be seen from the main road and the hostel's annexe nearby played the Glendarroch Hotel in the series, although the interior shots were recorded in the studio. Anyone wanting to stay at the hostel must be a member of the Youth Hostel Association.

In Luss itself, filming took place at the Highland Arts Gift Shop, which played Blair's Store, outside several cottages, at the church and at the manse. The ferry featured regularly and we often saw characters walking along the beach and on the pier. A farm at nearby Glenfruin was also featured. The nearby town of Helensburgh also appeared in the series for lots of shop scenes and the Coffee Club in Colquhoun Square also appeared regularly.

Sat nav references:

Brechin's Bar (G51 3DJ)
Coffee Club (G84 8AD)
Highland Arts Gift Shop (G83 8NZ)
Youth Hostel (G83 8RB)

Monarch of the Glen
Loch Laggan

Thanks to its views of the glorious Scottish Highlands and acres of breath taking scenery, *Monarch of the Glen* became unmissable Sunday night viewing between 2000 and 2005, with seven successful series making it one of the most popular television shows to come out of Scotland.

Even now, it is repeated all over the world and fans still make their way to stunning Loch Laggan, 16 miles south west of Newtonmore where much of the series was filmed, to catch a glimpse of all the landmarks which made *Monarch* so memorable.

Above: Privately-owned Ardverikie House, which was used as Glenbogle Castle in *Monarch of the Glen*.

The gorgeous setting for the fictional village of Glenbogle, with its mixture of eccentric and somehow innocent characters, was the village of Laggan and the splendid Glenbogle Castle, inhabited by the late Richard Briers' character Laird Hector Bogle, was played by the privately-owned Ardverikie House. The house can be seen – and photographed – from across the loch on the main Newtonmore to Fort William Road and indeed, many fans of the show still visit Ardverikie when they're in the area, despite it being off-limits to the general public.

During its heyday, *Monarch* brought a buzz to Ardverikie and Laggan as endless crew and cast members arrived to begin filming for several months at a time. Laggan locals and residents from a little further afield in the Badenoch areas of Newtonmore, Kingussie and Kincraig and further still, Strathspey (the area from Aviemore northwards), which were areas also used to shoot scenes, often became extras, boosting morale no end and ensuring everyone was happy with the whole *Monarch of the Glen* experience.

Production company Ecosse was given exclusive rights to the main part of Ardverikie House between February and October each year in order to film *Monarch*. During this period, the family were able to use a wing which had been renovated for them, then they moved back into the house once the film crews had left. The Gate Lodge, a holiday cottage belonging to the estate was often featured on the show. With its turret and picturesque setting at the entrance to the grounds, it is an ideal honeymoon retreat and is nearly always booked up months, if not years ahead. Another larger, self-catering estate property, Gallovie, doubled up as a bed and breakfast in the final series of Monarch. Again, it is possible to stay here – if you're lucky enough to book early.

Above: Richard Briers, Alastair Mackenzie and Susan Hampshire, the stars of *Monarch of the Glen*.

Sat nav references:

Ardverikie House (PH20 1BX)
The Glen Hotel (PH20 1DD)

There are also a further three self-catering properties available to rent on the Ardverikie estate. For further information, go to www.ardverikie.com The loch itself was also a feature of *Monarch*. A plane was sunk in its waters in one episode and of course, tragically Hector was blown up beside its banks. Susan Hampshire's character Molly was an artist and you may be interested to learn 'her' paintings were actually creations of a Newtonmore artist, David Fallows.

Local hotels often doubled up as Glenbogle premises and have become popular tourist spots as a result. For example, The Glen Hotel in Newtonmore, the car park of which sometimes popped up in *Monarch*, is worth a visit. Go to www.theglenhotel.co.uk to make a booking. As so many episodes were filmed in all, it's not surprising that a vast number of locations featured in *Monarch*. For further details go to www.monarchcountry.com

Shetland
Shetland

The stunning Shetland islands stand out as the major attraction in this police drama of the same name. Based on *Red Bones* by author Ann Cleeves, one of her Shetland quartet of novels, the pilot two-parter starred actor Douglas Henshall as returning native Shetlander DI Jimmy Perez and was the biggest drama production to ever be filmed locally.

ITV Studios, which made *Shetland* for the BBC, first filmed in July 2012 and found

Above: A stunning Shetland view.

the biggest problem was the lack of darkness, even at night. They were given rare permission to recreate the historic Up-Helly-Aa Viking Festival which normally takes place in darkest January but as they filmed over the summer solstice, they discovered it remains light around the clock.

While the isles of Shetland can't be described as picturesque, they have a rugged, windswept attraction, including over 1,700 miles of spectacular coastline. Both episodes of the drama managed to capture the uniqueness and wild beauty of the islands and there are high hopes of a boost to both tourism and future filming projects.

The key locations used in Shetland for the pilot were South Whiteness and parts of Lerwick, including Lerwick Harbour which is the principal commercial port for Shetland and also known as Britain's 'top port.' On the Mainland, a former council building in Barrhead doubled up as the interior of the police station while the exteriors were a real police station back in Lerwick.

Perez's on-screen house is actually to be found in the village of Kilbarchan near Glasgow, while some of the exteriors used are a waterfront property in Lerwick, the actual home of the character in the novel. Part of the Ayrshire coastline doubled up as Shetland, while a maritime museum in Ayr represented a museum in Irvine. See www.scottishmaritimemuseum.org for more details.

Sat nav references:

Lerwick Harbour (ZE1 0LL)

Taggart
Glasgow

Above: The late Mark McManus, the original star of *Taggart*.

In 2011, after 28 years ITV1 decided not to commission any further episodes of *Taggart* – which was the longest-running detective drama on television anywhere in the world - after a drop in viewing figures in the UK. However, the show remains hugely popular in Scotland so Scottish Television which made it, hasn't ruled out shooting further episodes.

The late Mark McManus starred as DCI Jim Taggart in the pilot episode screened in 1983 and he continued in the role as the tough, experienced cop until 1994 when he sadly passed away. Other actors subsequently joined and left the cast and by the time the latest episode to be screened was filmed in 2010, Blythe Duff, John Michie and Alex Norton were the main crime fighters at Maryhill Police Station.

Taggart was filmed primarily in the Glasgow area, although as you can imagine, in almost three decades, literally hundreds of locations were used so it would be a near impossible task to try and list each and every one of them here. An interesting fact is that Maryhill Police Station actually exists but the show was never shot there. Instead a number of different locations doubled up as the exterior of the police station which helps to explain why it didn't always look the same! The main police station and incident room featured in every episode were purpose-built sets and constructed in around a dozen or so locations since *Taggart* began. An industrial unit at Polmadie was the last set to be used.

Fans of *Taggart* enjoyed spotting some well-known attractions when they tuned into the show, such as the famous St Andrews Suspension Bridge which is located in the corner of Glasgow Green, furthest from the City Centre. The Bridge links Glasgow Green with St Adelphi Street on the other side of The Clyde.

Sat nav references:

Glasgow School of Art (G3 6RQ)
The People's Palace (G40 1AT)
Railway Station (G1 3SL)

Then there's Central Station, Glasgow's main railway station; The People's Palace which was built in 1898 as a cultural centre for the city's workers; The Winter Gardens, a large conservatory on the back of the Palace; Glasgow School of Art; George Square; Barrowland where a street market takes place every week; Scott Street, Buchanan Street and a string of restaurants and cafes.

Waterloo Road
Greenock

Above: The former Greenock Academy which is used for filming *Waterloo Road*.

The first seven series of this popular drama about a troubled comprehensive school was set in Rochdale, Manchester with filming taking place at the former Hill Top Primary School in Kirkholt.

Then in 2012 – six years after the first episodes were shot – Shed Productions, which produces the show for BBC1 through BBC Scotland, moved the set to the former Greenock Academy in Greenock.

The seventh series of *Waterloo Road* concluded in June 2012 with the headmaster Michael Byrne, played by Alec Newman, announcing he would be setting up a new school in Scotland with wealthy benefactor Lorraine Donnegan (Daniela Denby Ashe) and the first Scottish-set series was broadcast in the autumn of 2012.

Filming takes place for most of the year and a large production facility has been established at the new former Greenock Academy site including edit suites, a canteen, offices and make-up and costume rooms. Hill Top Primary School in Rochdale has since been demolished and the site is likely to be used for housing development.

Ireland, Jersey, Northern Ireland, France and Belgium

Ballykissangel
Bergerac
The Fall
Game of Thrones

Merlin
Monsignor Renard
The White Queen

Ballykissangel
Avoca, Ireland

Of course the town of Avoca in County Wicklow, which doubled on screen as the sleepy village of Ballykissangel, is actually in the Republic of Ireland and therefore obviously not part of Britain. Like a few other entries, it's included in this book simply because of the popularity of the BBC series

Above: (left) Assumpta Fitzgerald (Dervla Kirwan) *(centre)* The bridge on Avoca *(right)* Father Peter Clifford (Stephen Tompkinson).

and because it is within easy reach of the UK, as indeed are other shows filmed in Ireland and featured here.

The series began in 1996 and ran until 2001 and saw rookie English priest Father Peter Clifford, played by Stephen Tompkinson, arrive in Ballykissangel to take on a new job as the local curate. He became friends with local bar owner Assumpta, played by Dervla Kirwan, and soon wised up to the ways of the locals. He faced on-going battles with his immediate superior, wily old priest Father MacAnally, played by Niall Toiban, and local businessman Brian Quigley, played by Tony Doyle. After two series both Stephen and Dervla decided to quit the show and two new characters, Orla O'Connell, played by Victoria Smurfit and Sean Dillon, played by Lorcan Cranitch, were introduced to fill the gap and the series remained popular. The real-life locals of Avoca were delighted with the success of the show and the influx of visitors it has brought. Most interior scenes for *Ballykissangel*, apart from Hendley's shop which you can visit and has a fish and chip shop next door, were filmed in studios near Dublin but there's still plenty to see in Avoca. First stop might be Fitzgerald's, which played Fitzgerald's on screen (the name was changed for filming and the owners decided to stick with it) and where you're bound to get a warm welcome. About 100 yards up the road is St Mary and St Patrick Church, which doubled as St Joseph's. Then there is the local chemist which was used as the Post Office for filming. The locations for Quigley's House and Father Mac's are actually in Enniskerry, about 30 miles away. For more details see www.avoca.com and www.wicklow.ie

Bergerac
Jersey

For an island just nine miles long with a population of just 83,000, there were an awful lot of crimes committed on Jersey during the 1980s - well on screen at least. But far from putting visitors off, the success of the BBC detective series *Bergerac* brought visitors flocking to the island. The Jersey tourist authorities were delighted by the free publicity and they even hired the series' star, John Nettles, who played Triumph Roadster-driving Sergeant Jim Bergerac, to appear in their advertisements. No doubt history will repeat itself if plans revealed by the BBC in the Spring of 2013 for a remake of the drama come to fruition.

Most of the 45 square-mile island got a look in at some point during the series' ten-year run, which began in 1981. Lots of the locations used for the series are easy to see but not even a super-sleuth like Jim Bergerac could find the attractive stone cottage and farm that played his home in the first few series. For it was located in

Above: A young John Nettles as Jim Bergerac. *Opposite: (top)* Mont Orgueil Castle.

Queen's Valley in the east of the island and is now under hundreds of thousands of gallons of water as the whole valley was flooded in 1992 to make the new Queen's Valley Reservoir. Jim's ex-father-in-law, millionaire Charlie Hungerford, played by Terrance Alexander, lived in a luxury home portrayed by two different houses. The first was Noirmont

Manor, a beautiful house overlooking Belcroute Bay. The second was Windward House, which is private, and overlooks St Brelade's Bay. The Jersey Police Headquarters Jim worked from, the Bureau Des Estranges (Department for non Residents) was supposed to be in St Helier but is actually, Haute de la Garenne, a former childrens' home in the Parish of St Martin's in the east of the Island, which the BBC also used as a production base during filming. In reality, there is no such police department. Haute de la Garenne, now a centre for activity holidays, became the focus of a major police investigation in early 2008.

One of Jim's regular contacts was Diamante Lil, played by actress Mela White, who ran a restaurant and bar called The Royal Barge. In real life the restaurant was The Old Court House at St Aubin, a popular venue for both locals and visitors. Only the exterior was used for filming - the interior of The Royal Barge was a set built inside the Forum cinema in St Helier. Around the island dozens of places were used for filming the series. For example, the Round Tower, the most southerly German wartime fortification at Noirmont Point was used for an action sequence when a stunt man is thrown from the top of the tower to the rocks below after a fight.

The 11th Century Norman Church of St Brelade and its churchyard were used many times for weddings and funerals and the church hall played the headquarters of a dastardly medium in one episode. St Ouen's Manor, a private house which dates back to the 13th Century, was used repeatedly in the series in various guises as an art gallery and museum, as a French chateau, as the headquarters of a neo-fascist and as home to an eccentric millionaire, who was robbed by the ice maiden, Philippa Vale, played by Liza Goddard.

Beau Port, an attractive secluded beach, featured in an episode where Charlie Hungerford planned to build a huge hotel complex on the valley leading to it and cover the whole bay with a retractable glass dome. Needless to say, like many of Charlie's wilder ideas, it didn't happen, on or off screen. Mont Orgueil Castle was used just once in *Bergerac* in an episode about a German film star, played by Warren Clarke, who was making a movie in Jersey about the wartime German occupation. Jim later had a fight with the character and that took place on a large German bunker on the southern headland at St Ouen's Bay.

The beach at St Ouen's was featured many times and in one episode two young surfers found the body of a skin-diver there. Not far away, at St Mary's, on the road from St Ouen to Trinity, is the École Élémentaire, which played the school of Jim's daughter Kim. John Nettles ran into trouble with the real Jersey police during the filming of one episode when Jim chased a villain across St Brelade's Bay on a jet ski. Afterwards he was ticked off by an angry officer.

Sat nav references:

Forum cinema (JE2 4SU)
Haute de la Garenne (JE3 6DU)
Mont Orgueil Castle (JE3 6ET)
The Old Court House (JE3 8AB)
St Ouen's Manor (JE3 2HR)

The Fall
Belfast, Northern Ireland

The BBC's acclaimed 2013 serial killer drama *The Fall*, which starred Gillian Anderson as Detective Superintendent Stella Gibson, made gripping but sometimes uncomfortable viewing. Filmed in Belfast, it showed the full range of the city's architecture, both old and new.

Here are the main places used for filming: Belfast International Airport was — surprise, surprise - the airport, the Waterfront Hall was the location of the police press conference relating to the Sarah Kaye murder, W5 science centre at the Odyssey Complex was used for the

Above: Gillian Anderson as Detective Superintendent Stella Gibson in *The Fall*.

policing board boardroom and New Lodge Estate was where Stella Gibson met the detective who was later murdered.

The Botanic Gardens played themselves, Victoria Park was where Spector jogged and also escaped from the Annie Brawley crime scene in the water, the Malmaison Hotel was where German businessmen were entertained by prostitutes and a house in Ulsterville Avenue was used as the exterior of Spector's House.

The Hilton Hotel was where Gibson stayed and was doorstepped by a journalist in the restaurant, Belfast Metropolitan College – both inside and out - was used as the main police station and as Spector's place of work.

Stranmillis Primary School was where Spector's children went to school, the pool at the Holiday Inn was where Gibson swam, Whiteabbey

Above: Detective Superintendent Stella Gibson (Gillian Anderson) at a crime scene in *The Fall.*

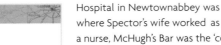

Sat nav references:
Botanic Gardens (BT7 1LP)
The Hilton Hotel (BT1 3LP)
Malmaison Hotel (BT1 3GH)
Whiteabbey Hospital (BT37 9RH)

Hospital in Newtownabbey was where Spector's wife worked as a nurse, McHugh's Bar was the 'coppers pub' and Victoria Square was where the scene with the phone call between Spector and Gibson at the end of the last episode was filmed.

Game of Thrones
Northern Ireland

This epic fantasy television drama, based on George R.R Martin's *A Song of Ice and Fire* series of novels follows the story of seven noble families fighting for control of the mythical world of Westros. It was first screened in the UK in April 2011 and has become one of Sky Atlantic's most popular shows.

Above: Ballintoy Harbour, dressed for filming of *Game of Thrones.*

In the opening scene of episode one, series one, the Northern lands sequence was filmed at Tollymore Forest Park at the foot of the Mourne Mountains (www.nidirect.gov.uk/forests) and it's there that we first encountered the White Walkers and the men of the Night's Watch riding through the snow. This location was also used in episode four of series three where Theon Greyjoy, of the Iron Islands, was allowed to escape from the Dreadfort, just to be chased through the forest on horseback by Ramsay Bolton.

Castle Ward, a National Trust house in Strangford, in County Down, was used for the exterior of Winterfell and the land surrounding the castle of the North, the home of the Stark family. A particularly memorable scene was the arrival of King Robert Baratheon and his retinue at Winterfell. The location for Winterfell moved in series two after it was burnt down by Ramsay Bolton. For the pilot episode Doune Castle in Scotland was used.

The location for Robb Stark's camp in series two was at Audley's Field, beside Castle Ward. As their journey continued to Kings Landing, they crossed the river by Inch Abbey, a ruin on the River Quoile near Downpatrick, County Down. The river was the location for the lands surrounding Riverrun, home of the Tully family and was also used for Hoster Tully's funeral scene.

The Dark Hedges, a unique stretch of the Bregagh Road near Armoy, was used in series two where Arya Stark and Gendry were on the road on the back of a cart. This famous road is one of the most photographed natural phenomena in Northern Ireland. The extraordinary beech trees were planted in the 1700s and are said to be haunted by a "grey lady".

The burning of the seven gods in series two, during which viewers were introduced to Melisandre, the Red Priestess of the Lord of Light, was filmed at Downhill Strand, a stunning beach in County

Right: (top) **Game of Throne statues at Downhill Strand,** *(middle)* **The remarkable Dark Hedges of Armoy,** *(bottom)* **Ballintoy Harbour which plays Lordsport Harbour.**

Above: Tents erected on the cliffs at Ballintoy.

Londonderry.

Murlough Bay in County Antrim was used as Pyke, part of Iron Islands, home of the Greyjoys and featured when Theon Greyjoy landed back home on Pyke. Murlough Bay was also used in the scene where Stanis and Renly Baratheon talk but failed to agree who was the rightful king and where Davos Seaworth was rescued after being shipwrecked on a rocky island. Beautiful Ballintoy harbour and beach doubled as Lordsport Harbour in Pyke.

Scenes of Renly Baratheon's camp, Storm's End, was filmed at Larrybane, which is a plateau above the Giant's Causeway with fabulous views around the coast. The memorable scene in episode four of series two, when Davos Seaworth landed Melisandre at night near Renly Baratheon's camp to give birth to the shadow baby, was filmed at Cushendun Caves in County Antrim.

The stunning Mourne Mountains were used in series three when Bran Stark, Rickon Stark, Hordor and Osha met Jojen and Meera Reed on the road to The Wall. The exterior of the outlaw's hideout Hallow Hill, where Arya Stark, Gendry and Hot Pie met Beric Dondarrion and his brotherhood, was filmed at Pollnagollum Cave and Waterfall in County Fermanagh.

Titanic Studios in Belfast – which, as the name suggests are on the site for the shipyard where the doomed liner was built, were used for filming of interior scenes of locations such as Winterfell – but aren't open to the public. Although most of *Game of Thrones* is filmed in Northern Ireland, other scenes have been filmed in Iceland, Morocco, Malta and Croatia.

France
Merlin

The beautiful Château de Pierrefonds (right) in northern France is obviously not in Britain but as the setting for the BBC's popular series *Merlin*, which ran from 2008 to 2012, we thought it was worth including. A castle has existed on the site since the 12th Century and in addition to playing Camelot in *Merlin* it also appeared in the film *The Messenger: The Story of Joan of Arc*.

Monsignor Renard

Although the 2000 ITV drama *Monsignor Renard* wasn't filmed in Britain either, the location for it is included here because it is easy to reach. The late John Thaw starred in the four-part drama as a Catholic priest drawn into the French resistance while living in a town under Nazi occupation. The drama was filmed in the beautiful town of Saint-Valery-sur-Somme (right) which overlooks Somme Bay, famous as the site where William the Conqueror assembled his fleet before sailing over to England in 1066.

Belgium
The White Queen

The epic BBC Wars of the Roses drama *The White Queen*, which starred Max Irons, Rebecca Ferguson (right) and Janet McTeer, might have been set in medieval England but the 10-part series was actually filmed in Belgium. And makers Company Pictures made full use of the some of the country's finest historical buildings in the blockbuster series.

Among the key locations used were St Martin's Cathedral, Ypres, which played Westminster Abbey and stunning Gravensteen in Ghent, which doubled as Henry Tudor's ancestral home Pembroke Castle and also as part of Warwick Castle.

The Belfry, Bruges and St Pieter's Abbey, St Pieter's Cathedral and St Bavo's Abbey, all in Ghent, were used as Westminster Palace exteriors and Stadhuis, Bruges' town hall played Westminster Palace's main hall.

Rubenskasteel in Elewijt was used as Norwich Cathedral and Kasteel van Rumbeke was Grafton Manor, childhood home of Elizabeth Woodville. The oak tree where Elizabeth and Edward IV first met was in Kasteelpark van Edingen and the Battle of Bosworth was shot at Ryckevelde Woods in Damme.

More from Splendid Books

Only Fools and Horses - The Official Inside Story
By Steve Clark, Foreword by Theo Paphitis

This book takes us behind the scenes to reveal the secrets of the hit show and is fully authorised by the family of its writer John Sullivan. This engaging tribute contains interviews with the show's stars and members of the production team, together with rarely seen pictures. Written by bestselling author Steve Clark, the only writer on set for the filming of Only Fools and Horses, The Green Green Grass and Rock & Chips, this book gives a fascinating and unique insight into this legendary series.

£9.99 (paperback)

The Official Only Fools and Horses Quiz Book
Compiled by Dan Sullivan and Jim Sullivan, Foreword by John Sullivan

Now you can test your knowledge of the legendary sitcom in The Official Only Fools and Horses Quiz Book, which is packed with more than 1,000 brain-teasers about the show. Plus there's an episode guide and an exclusive foreword by the show's creator and writer John Sullivan, who reveals some of the mystery behind the much-loved series and just how he came up with some of television's most memorable moments.

£7.99 (paperback)

The Wit and Wisdom of Only Fools and Horses
Compiled by Dan Sullivan, Foreword by Sir David Jason OBE

The crème de menthe of the hilarious one-liners from Only Fools and Horses have been brought together for the first time in The Wit and Wisdom of Only Fools and Horses. Re-live all Del, Rodney, Grandad, Uncle Albert, Boycie, Trigger and the rest of the gang's funniest and most memorable lines. Compiled by Dan Sullivan, son of Only Fools and Horses creator John Sullivan, and with a foreword by Sir David Jason OBE, this triffic book is a lovely jubbly, pukka, 42-carat gold-plated bargain.

£4.99 (paperback)

FREE
DELIVERY
ON ALL
ORDERS

Splendid
BOOKS

To order:
By phone: 0845 625 3045
or online: www.splendidbooks.co.uk

By post: Send a cheque (payable to Splendid Books Limited) to: Splendid Books Limited, The Old Hambledon Racecourse Centre, Sheardley Lane, Droxford, Hampshire SO32 3QY UK

About the authors

Steve Clark

Steve Clark has been specialising in behind-the-scenes reports on television programmes for more than twenty years. He is author of *The Only Fools and Horses Story* (BBC Books, 1998), *The World of Jonathan Creek* (BBC Books, 1999), *On Set* (Blake Publishing, 1999) and *Captain Corelli's Mandolin - The Illustrated Film Companion* (Headline, 2001) and *Only Fools and Horses – The Official Inside Story*. He lives in Hampshire with his wife and their two children.

"Steve Clark's book The Official Inside Story is the definitive history of Only Fools and Horses"
Sir David Jason

 Follow Steve on Twitter **@steveclarkuk** • **www.steveclark.co.uk**

Shoba Vazirani

Shoba Vazirani has been a journalist for more than 25 years and has extensive experience in both local and national press and broadcasting. She helped launch Sky News and was Deputy TV Editor of *The Sun*. She lives in Surrey with her husband and their three children.

 Follow Shoba on Twitter **@shobavazirani**

Updates

The authors would be pleased to hear from readers with details of new locations and updates on existing ones. Please contact Steve Clark at stevelg@splendidbooks.co.uk or Shoba Vazirani at shobalg@splendidbooks.co.uk or via the address on page 6. For news about filming locations and new productions go to **www.whereitsfilmed.com**

 Follow The British Television Location Guide on Twitter **@tvlocationguide**

 Follow Splendid Books on Twitter **@splendidbooks**

Acknowledgements

The authors are indebted to all those who helped with the preparation of this book especially: (alphabetically): Simon Allen, Heather Armitage, Ralph Assheton, Andrew Bainbridge, Natasha Bayford, Kevin Bell, Jenny Bradley, Rupert Bray, Kay Breeze, Richard Brown, Janet Bruton, Joseph Cairns, James Caterer, Rebecca Channon, Nicola Cheriton-Sutton, Barry Clark, Nicola Clark, Andrea Collitt, Nigel Crisp, Rikke Dakin, Harvey Edgington, Thomas Elgood, Jenny Ellenger, Stephen Elliott, Claire Evans, Pat Eyre, Midge Ferguson, Fiona Frankham, John Friend Newman, Chris Fulcher, Robbie Gibbs, Nuala Giblin, Tryphena Greenwood, Dee Gregson, Mark Grimwade, Paul Gulliver, Javis Gurr, Martin Henderson, Arron Hendy, Michael Higson, Linda Hill, David Hitchcock, Andi Hollingsworth, Joel Holmes, Kerry Ixer, Nicky James, Christina Joyce, David Kellick, Stacey Killon, Jamie Lengyel, Billy Lintell, Caroline Lowsley-Williams, Jamie Lovelace, Alice Lumley, Donald Mackinnon, Esther Mars, Nick Marshall, Richard May, Natalie Moore, Michael More-Molyneaux, Andy Morgan, Hayley Morgan, Jess Newbould, Catriona Newman, John Friend Newman, Karen Nicholson, Robert Noble, Adrian Notter, Michele Notter, Emily Ogden, Frances Pardell, Paul Pearson, Naomi Phillipson, Katherine Powley, Berenice Ray, Keith Righton, Iwan Roberts, Theresa Robson, Owain Rowlands, Helen Saunders, Keith Simmonds, Sandra Simmonds, Andrew Sharpe, Annabel Silk, Patrick Smith, Andrew Stables, Lady Angela Stucley, Tony Tarran, Gillian Thompson, Chris Tinsley, Sarah Upton, Paul Vigay, Jenni Wagstaffe, Pete Ware, Hugh Warren, Luc Webster, Rick Weston, Pam White, Julie Whiteside, Susan Wilks, Gareth Williams, Andrew Wilson, Brett Wilson and Stuart Wright.

Selected references & useful further reading

Bergerac's Jersey by John Nettles (BBC Books, 1988), The Bill - The Inside Story of British Television's Most Successful Police Series by Tony Lynch (Boxtree, 1991), Doctor Who Magazine, *The Only Fools and Horses Story* by Steve Clark (BBC Books, 1998), Only Fools and Horses - The Official Inside Story by Steve Clark (Splendid Books, 2011), *The World of Inspector Morse* by Christopher Bird (Boxtree, 1998), *The World of Jonathan Creek* by Steve Clark (BBC Books, 1999) and • www.whereitsfilmed.com • www.doctorwholocations.net • www.english-heritage.org. uk • www.nationaltrust.org.uk

Index

Photo credits

The authors are also grateful to the photographers and companies who have kindly allowed their pictures to be used. They are credited below:

Jacket front: Call The Midwife: Neal Street Productions; Broadchurch: Kudos Productions / ITV; Doc Martin: ITV/Rex Features; Midsomer Murders: © Bentley Productions; Downton Abbey: ITV/Rex Features

Jacket rear: Mr Selfridge: ITV; Foyle's War: © 2013 Foyles War 8 Productions; Endeavour: Mammoth Screen

Pages 2-3: www.dragon-pictures.com; pages 4-5: Ian Lowe www.showmeyoursmile.co.uk; page 7: Call The Midwife: Neal Street Productions • Midsomer Murders: © Bentley Productions; page 8: Call The Midwife: Neal Street Productions • Midsomer Murders: © Bentley Productions • Endeavour: Mammoth Screen • Mr Selfridge: ITV • Broadchurch: Kudos Productions / ITV • Downton Abbey: ITV/Rex Features • Last Tango in Halifax: Red Production Company / BBC • The White Queen: © Company Pictures / ALL3MEDIA • Doc Martin: Michael Saunders; page 9: Andy Dakin; page 10: Kineta Hill • Kudos Productions / ITV; pages 11 & 12: Kudos Productions / ITV; page 13: Lynda Morris • Martine van Meerbeeck; pages 14-15: David Betteridge www. dhbphotography.co.uk; page 16: Alan Davies www. bigaldavies.co.uk; page 17: Steve Clark; page 18: Michael Saunders; page 19: Michael Saunders http://youtu.be/LMeVTZb3u5I • Andy Dakin; page 20: Steven Diffey; page 21: Rex Features • David Betteridge www.dhbphotography.co.uk; page 22: Chavenage; page 23: Steve Clark • www.solentnews.biz • www.scopefeatures. com; pages 24: South West News Service (SWNS) • Rick Weston; page 25: South West News Service (SWNS); page 26: Owen Benson www.owenbenson.co.uk; page 27: © English Heritage Photo Library • Kevin Carson; page 28: Lady Stucley • Steve Bevan; page 29: Mark Bourdillon • www.warnerleisurehotels.co.uk; page 30: ITV/Rex Features • Ian Garfield; page 31: Neal Street Productions; page 32: ITV/Rex Features • Richard Stead; page 33: ITV/Rex Features; page 34: Caitlin Ferguson-Mir www. photoexpedition.co.uk • Eagle Eyes; page 35: Neal Street Productions; page 36: Mike Gwilliams; page 37: Neal Street Productions • Matt Smith; page 38: ITV / Rex Features; page 39: ITV / Rex Features; page 40: Kathy Cook; pages 41 & 42: ITV / Rex Features; page 43: Ron Hanko • John Sandys • Rex Features • Mark Fanthorpe; page 44: Bob Mazzer www.bobmazzer.com • Vincent Hoban; page 45: © 2013 Foyles War 8 Productions; page 46: Jason M Kelly • Bob Mazzer; page 47: Bob Mazzer; page 48: Rex Features; Page 49: Tony Larkin / Rex Features • Chester Tugwell; page 50: Tony Larkin / Rex Features • Steve Clark; page 51: © Bentley Productions; page 52: © John Ward, Aston Rowant, Oxfordshire; page 53: © Bentley Productions; page 54: David Betteridge • © John Ward, Aston Rowant; pages 55 & 56: ITV; page 57: John Thorne • Thomas Cogley; page 58: © English Heritage • Its Lefty; page 59: David Purton www.pictures4partners.co.uk • St Albans Register Office • Andy Penney; page 60: Debbie Borrett • Adrian Porter www.Ymzala.net; page 61: Courtesy of the BBC; page 62: Terry Moran • Eagle Eyes; page 63: Steve Clark • Courtesy of the BBC; page 64: Dorset Echo • Royal Oak; page 65: Jamie Barras; page 66: Yusuf Solley; page 67: Eagle Eyes; page 68: Jamie Barras; page 69: Eagle Eyes; page 70: Lynford Hall Hotel • Edward Wing / Rex Features; page 71: Stuart Wright / The Dad's Army Appreciation Society • Nick Ford www.nickpix. co.uk; page 72: Nick Ford; page 73: Eagle Eyes • Albanpix Ltd/Rex Features • Steve Clark; page 74: © NTPL / Ray Hallett • Michael J Davis; page 75: Mammoth Screen; page 76: Rockingham Castle; pages 77-79: Mammoth Screen; page 80: Courtesy of www.britainonview.com • ITV / Rex Features; page 81: Courtesy of www.britainonview. com; page 82: Steve Poole / Scope Features; page 85: Kingpin Media; page 84: Minke Spiro / Rex Features • Lincolnshire County Council; page 86: © Andrew Tryner / English Heritage Photo Library • ITV / Rex Features; pages 86 & 87: Charlie Morton; page 88: © NTPL / Rupert Truman • Roger Nichol; page 89: Mark Campbell / Rex Features; page 91: www.dragonpictures. com; page 92: Rex Features; page 93: www.walesnews.com; page 94: Laura Blakemore • Alan Peters; page 95: The News, Portsmouth; page 96: Allan Ballard / www.scopefeatures.com; page 97: Darren Griffiths • www.llechwedd-slate-caverns.co.uk; page 98 & 99 www. portmeirion-village.com; page 100: Rex Features; page 101: Last Tango in Halifax: Red Production Company/BBC; page 102: Liverpool Film Office • Steve Drewry; page 103: aerial view by www. airviews.info • ITV / Rex Features; pages 104-106: Last Tango in Halifax: Red Production Company / BBC; pages 107 & 108: www. cavendish-press.co.uk; page 109: www.cavendish-press.co.uk • Joseph Cairns • © NTPL / Matthew Antrobus; page 110: TVTimes / www.scopefeatures. com; pages 111-114: Ian Lowe www. showmeyoursmile.co.uk; page 115: ITV; page 116: Rex Features • Ribble Valley Borough Council; page 117: Mike Kipling www. mikekipling.com • Karen Lewis; page 118: Karen Lewis • Tim Green; pages 119 & 120: Keith Simmonds www.glendalehouse.co.uk; page 121: © NTPL / Joe Cornish • © NTPL / Andrew Butler; page 122: Rex Features; page 123: Kirklees Council • Joyce Turner • Helen Ibbotson • Richard Brown; page 124: Mark Dyson; page 125: ITV; page 126: Antony Cairns • Newcastle City Council; page 127: Paul Beentjes; page 128 Argyll and Bute Council; page 129: Barbara Jones; page 130: www.visitscotland.com; page 131: Brian Moody / Scope Features • David Gifford www.davegifford.co.uk; page 132: www.scopefeatures.com • Zak Harrison; page 133: Amanda Killen; page 134: Chris Craymer / www. scopefeatures.com • World Productions Ltd / BBC Photo Library • Chris Hill / www.discoverireland.com; page 135: www.jersey. com • © Fall Productions Ltd. 2013; page 136: © Fall Productions Ltd. 2013 • Helen McCall; page 137: Amanda Killen • Helen McCall • Aidan Loughridge; page 138: Rick Gregg; page 139: Mark Andrews • Steve Clark • The White Queen: © Company Pictures / ALL3MEDIA.

Road sign graphics: Crown copyright • Jacket and page 7 maps: Ordnance Survey